VIEWPOINT

STUDENT'S BOOK 2A

MICHAEL MCCARTHY
JEANNE MCCARTEN
HELEN SANDIFORD

CAMBRIDGE
UNIVERSITY PRESS

CAMBRIDGE
UNIVERSITY PRESS

University Printing House, Cambridge CB2 8BS, United Kingdom

One Liberty Plaza, 20th Floor, New York, NY 10006, USA

477 Williamstown Road, Port Melbourne, VIC 3207, Australia

4843/24, 2nd Floor, Ansari Road, Daryaganj, Delhi – 110002, India

79 Anson Road, #06–04/06, Singapore 079906

Cambridge University Press is part of the University of Cambridge.

It furthers the University's mission by disseminating knowledge in the pursuit of education, learning and research at the highest international levels of excellence.

www.cambridge.org
Information on this title: www.cambridge.org/9781107601543

Student's Book first published 2014
Online Course 2016
20 19 18 17 16 15 14 13 12 11 10 9 8 7 6 5 4

Printed in Great Britain by CPI Group (UK) Ltd, Croydon CR0 4YY

A catalog record for this publication is available from the British Library.

ISBN 978-0-521-13189-6 Student's Book
ISBN 978-1-107-60154-3 Student's Book A
ISBN 978-1-107-60155-0 Student's Book B
ISBN 978-1-107-60631-9 Workbook
ISBN 978-1-107-57205-8 Workbook A
ISBN 978-1-107-57213-3 Workbook B
ISBN 978-1-107-60156-7 Teacher's Edition with Assessment Audio CD/CD-ROM
ISBN 978-1-107-66132-5 Class Audio CDs (4)
ISBN 978-1-107-67577-3 Presentation Plus
ISBN 978-1-107-56841-9 Student's Book with Online Workbook
ISBN 978-1-107-56846-4 Student's Book with Online Workbook A
ISBN 978-1-107-56849-5 Student's Book with Online Workbook B
ISBN 978-1-107-56808-2 Student's Book with Online Course (includes Online Workbook)
ISBN 978-1-107-56809-9 Student's Book with Online Course (includes Online Workbook) A
ISBN 978-1-107-56810-5 Student's Book with Online Course (includes Online Workbook) B

Additional resources for this publication at www.cambridge.org/viewpoint

Authors' acknowledgements

The authors would like to thank the entire team of professionals who have contributed their expertise to creating *Viewpoint 2*. We appreciate you all, including those we have not met. Here we would like to thank the people with whom we have had the most personal, day-to-day contact through the project. In particular, Michael Poor, who skillfully and sensitively edited the material and dedicated so much time and professional expertise to help us improve it; Mary Vaughn for her usual sage advice on our syllabus and her excellent contributions to the pronunciation materials; Dawn Elwell for her superb production skills; copy editor Karen Davy for checking through the manuscripts; Sue Aldcorn and Arley Gray for their work on creating the Teacher's Edition; Helen Tiliouine, Therese Naber and Janet Gokay, for creating and editing the testing program; Cristina Zurawski and Graham Skerritt for their comments on some of the early drafts, Mary McKeon, for her series oversight and project management; Melissa Struck for her help on the workbook and project management; Rossita Fernando and Jennifer Pardilla for their roles on the Workbook, Class Audio, and Video Program; Catherine Black for her support on the answer keys and audio scripts and deft handling of the Online Workbook; Tyler Heacock and Kathleen Corley, and their friends and family for the recordings they made, which fed into the materials; Ann Fiddes for corpus support and access to the English Profile wordlists; Dr. Cynan Ellis Evans for the interview on page 45, and Kristen Ulmer for the interview which is reported on page 55.

We would also like to express our deep appreciation to Bryan Fletcher and Sarah Cole, who started the *Viewpoint* project with incredible vision and drive; and Janet Aitchison for her continued support.

Finally, we would like to thank each other for getting through another project together! In addition, Helen Sandiford would like to thank her husband, Bryan, and her daughters for their unwavering support.

In addition, a great number of people contributed to the research and development of *Viewpoint*. The authors and publishers would like to extend their particular thanks to the following for their valuable insights and suggestions.

Reviewers and consultants:
Elisa Borges and Samara Camilo Tomé Costa from **Instituto Brasil-Estados Unidos**, Rio de Janeiro, Brazil; Deborah Iddon from **Harmon Hall** Cuajimalpa, México; and Chris Sol Cruz from **Suncross Media LLC**. Special thanks to Sedat Cilingir, Didem Mutçalıoğlu, and Burcu Tezvan from **İstanbul Bilgi Üniversitesi**, İstanbul, Turkey for their invaluable input in reviewing both the Student's Book and Workbook.

The authors and publishers would also like to thank our design and production teams at Nesbitt Graphics, Inc., Page 2, LLC, and New York Audio Productions.

Cambridge University Press staff and advisors:
Mary Lousie Baez, Jeff Chen, Seil Choi, Vincent Di Blasi, Julian Eynon, Maiza Fatureto, Keiko Hirano, Chris Hughes, Peter Holly, Tomomi Katsuki, Jeff Krum, Christine Lee, John Letcher, Vicky Lin, Hugo Loyola, Joao Madureira, Alejandro Martinez, Daniela A. Meyer, Devrim Ozdemir, Jinhee Park, Gabriela Perez, Panthipa Rojanasuworapong, Luiz Rose, Howard Siegelman, Satoko Shimoyama, Ian Sutherland, Alicione Soares Tavares, Frank Vargas, Julie Watson, Irene Yang, Jess Zhou, Frank Zhu.

Viewpoint Level 2A *Scope and sequence*

	Functions / Topics	Grammar	Vocabulary	Conversation strategies	Speaking naturally
Unit 1 **A great read** pages 10–19	• Talk about types of literature, reading habits, and favorite authors. • Discuss the pros and cons of reading and writing blogs. • Analyze and interpret a poem.	• Use auxiliary verbs, *to, one,* and *ones* to avoid repeating words and phrases.	• Idiomatic expressions for understanding (*I can't make heads or tails of it*) and remembering (*It's on the tip of my tongue)* • Synonyms (*enduring - lasting*)	• Use stressed auxiliary verbs (*do, does*) before main verbs to add emphasis. • Use *if so* to mean "if this is true", and *if not* to mean "if this is not true."	• Stressing auxiliaries for emphasis *page 138*
Unit 2 **Technology** pages 20–29	• Talk about technology and its impact on your life. • Discuss the issue of privacy vs. security. • Evaluate the pros and cons of modern conveniences. • Discuss how you respond to new technologies.	• Add information to nouns with different types of expressions. • Use two-part conjunctions like *either . . . or* to combine ideas.	• Compound adjectives to describe technology (*high-speed, energy-efficient*) • Suffixes (*innova**tion**, radic**al***)	• Use adverbs like *predictably* and *apparently* to express what you predict, expect, etc. • Emphasize that something is impossible with *can't / couldn't possibly.*	• Stress in noun phrases *page 138*
Unit 3 **Society** pages 30–39	• Talk about different social pressures that you and others face. • Discuss the challenges of starting college and other new experiences. • Discuss how children put pressure on parents. • Evaluate gender differences in language.	• Use participle clauses to link events and add information about time or reason. • Add emphasis with *so . . . that, such . . . that, even,* and *only.*	• Expressions with *take* (*take advantage of, take credit for*) • Synonyms (*often – frequently; show – reveal*)	• Express a contrasting view with expressions like *having said that* and *then again.* • Use *even so* and *even then* to introduce a contrasting idea.	• Stress in expressions of contrast *page 139*
Checkpoint 1 Units 1–3 pages 40–41					

Listening	Reading	Writing	Vocabulary notebook	Grammar extra
The blogosphere • A presenter shares statistics about blogging. *My interpretation is . . .* • Someone gives an interpretation of a poem.	*A brief history of poetry* • An article about different types of poetry through history	• Write a review of a book you have enjoyed. • Describe, evaluate, and recommend a book. • Coordinate adjectives. • Avoid errors with *yet.*	*Heads or tails* • Think of situations when you can use certain idioms.	• More on auxiliary verbs to avoid repetition • *too, either, so, neither,* and *(to) do so* • More on using *to* to avoid repeating verb phrases • More on *one* /*ones* to avoid repeating countable nouns *pages 144–145*
Privacy or convenience? • Two friends discuss privacy and fingerprinting. *How do you multitask?* • Three conversations about multitasking	*As technology changes, so do adoption life cycles.* • An article about the willingness of consumers to invest in new technology	• Write a report about Internet use. • Describe graphs, charts, and tables. • Describe and compare statistics. • Avoid errors with *as can be seen*, etc.	*High-tech gadgets* • Use compound adjectives with nouns to say something true about your life.	• Adjectives after nouns • Negative phrases after nouns • More on two-part conjunctions • Two-part conjunctions with phrases and clauses *pages 146–147*
It's an issue . . . • Two people discuss the challenges when kids become more independent. *Language and gender* • A professor introduces a course on language and gender.	*Spring semester courses in Language and Society* • Course outlines of classes about language and society	• Write an evaluation of a course. • Plan and write an evaluative report. • Express results in writing. • Avoid errors with *therefore.*	*Take credit!* • Write sentences that paraphrase the meaning of new expressions.	• Clauses with prepositions and conjunctions + *-ing* • Passive forms of participle and time clauses • More on *so* and *such* • More on *even* and *only* *pages 148–149*

Checkpoint 1 Units 1–3 pages 40–41

	Functions / Topics	Grammar	Vocabulary	Conversation strategies	Speaking naturally
Unit 4 **Amazing world** pages 42–51	• Talk about the natural world. • Present information about a member of the animal kingdom. • Consider the impact that humans have on nature.	• Use future perfect forms to talk about the past in the future. • Use prepositions and prepositional phrases to combine ideas.	• Expressions to describe the behavior of wildlife (*hibernate, predator*) • Suffixes with *-able* (*remarkable, valuable*)	• Use expressions like *What's more* to add and focus on new ideas. • Use *in any case* and *in any event* to strengthen arguments and reach conclusions.	• Stress in adding expressions *page 139*
Unit 5 **Progress** pages 52–61	• Talk about inventions, progress, and human achievements. • Evaluate the motivation of people who are driven to perform dangerous feats. • Discuss the pros and cons of research. • Discuss inventions and innovations.	• Use adverbs with continuous and perfect forms of the passive. • Use past modals with the passive.	• More formal adjectives (*obsolete, portable*) • Adjectives into nouns (*convenient – convenience; easy – ease*)	• Use expressions like *Let's put it this way* to make a point. • Use expressions like *Maybe (not), Absolutely (not),* and *Not necessarily* in responses.	• Stress in expressions *page 140*
Unit 6 **Business studies** pages 62–71	• Talk about business and retail. • Consider the motivations behind shopping habits. • Evaluate the benefits of online and instore shopping. • Present the advantages of big business and small business.	• Use relative clauses that begin with pronouns or prepositions. • Use *some, any, other, others,* and *another* to refer to people and things.	• Verbs that mean *attract* and *deter* (*entice, discourage*) • Adjectives (*malicious, vulnerable*)	• Use negative and tag questions to persuade others of your point of view. • Use *granted* to concede points.	• Prepositions in relative clauses *page 140*
Checkpoint 2 Units 4–6 pages 72–73					

Listening	Reading	Writing	Vocabulary notebook	Grammar extra
The Antarctic • An expert answers questions about Antarctica. *The genius of the natural world* • A presenter shares ideas about how biomimicry could solve problems.	*How nature inspires science – a look at some notable inventions* • An article about how nature inspires innovation	• Write a persuasive essay about an environmental concern. • Use academic prepositions and impersonal *one.* • Avoid errors with *upon.*	*Golden eggs* • Notice the use of specialized vocabulary in general English or in idioms.	• More on the future perfect • The future perfect for predictions and assumptions • Formal prepositional expressions • More on *the fact that;* prepositions + perfect forms *pages 150–151*
Kristen Ulmer – a world-class extreme skier • A reporter relates her conversation with Kristen Ulmer. *What's the point of research?* • Two people discuss the benefits and drawbacks of research.	*Invention: inspired thinking or accidental discovery?* • An article about how inventions come about	• Write an opinion essay about technological progress. • Compare and contrast arguments. • Use *it* clauses + passive to say what people think. • Avoid errors with *affect* and *effect.*	*Old or ancient?* • Learn synonyms to express basic concepts in formal writing.	• Adverbs in present and past passive verb phrases • Adverbs in perfect verb phrases • Adverbs and past modal verb phrases • Questions with passive past modals *pages 152–153*
Too good to be true? • Four consumer experts talk about special promotions. *The top threats* • A business expert discusses the risks of running a business.	*Data leakage – Are you protected?* • An article about keeping a business's information secure	• Write a report on data security. • Use modals to avoid being too assertive and to make recommendations. • Use expressions to describe cause (*This may be the result of . . .*). • Avoid errors with *can* and *could.*	*It's tempting.* • Write word family charts.	• Pronouns and numbers in relative clauses • Nouns in relative clauses • *other, every other, other than* • More on *another* *pages 154–155*

Checkpoint 2 Units 4–6 pages 72–73

Unit 1

A great read

In Unit 1, you . . .

- talk about literature, reading habits, and favorite authors.
- avoid repeating words by using auxiliary verbs, *to*, and *one(s)*.
- use auxiliary verbs for emphasis.
- use *if so* and *if not* instead of repeating ideas.

Lesson A *Memoirs*

1 Grammar in context

A **Read the six-word memoirs below. Can you guess the story behind each memoir?**

Who are you – in six words? Our readers wrote their autobiographies in just six words.

ⓐ 
Lindsay
Former accountant now wears chef's apron.

ⓒ 
Yoshio
Traveled everywhere. Saw everything. Sadly, broke.

ⓔ 
Tim
Every 10 years, I reinvent myself.

ⓑ 
Dave
Happily raising three beautiful kids. Exhausted!

ⓓ 
Sasha
Studied hard. Good degree. No job.

ⓕ 
Stella
The good child – until I wasn't!

B CD 1.02 **Listen. Which memoir is each person talking about? Write the letters a–f.**

1. _____ "Like me he seems family oriented. He's obviously enjoying family life – as I am. But he finds it hard. Most people do. I know my sister does. She has three children – all under six!"
2. _____ "Well, she obviously changed careers – a lot of people do these days. But it sounds like she took a risk by choosing a career that's not as lucrative, which is what I did, too. I hope it works out for her. It did for me, but for some people it doesn't."
3. _____ "I'd say this person worked hard in college, which most students do. But it's too bad he or she hasn't gotten any work. I know a lot of graduates who haven't. It's so discouraging."
4. _____ "Sounds like me. I was the perfect kid – made my bed, ate my vegetables, and my brothers never did. At college I went wild, as a lot of kids do. Dyed my hair pink . . ."
5. _____ "This person clearly likes change. Actually, I'm thinking of making a big change in my life. I'm contemplating volunteering. I think it's a great idea, but my family doesn't for some reason."
6. _____ "He must have traveled all over. I'd love to do that. I haven't been abroad once. Most of my friends haven't either. I'm saving up for a trip, and so is one of my friends. So maybe soon."

About you

C Pair work **Discuss the questions below. Do you agree?**

Which memoir writer in your view . . .

- seems happiest?
- might be least satisfied?
- has had the best experiences?
- has taken the most risks?
- has had the best education?
- is the most successful?
- seems the most interesting person?
- is most like someone you know?

2 Grammar Avoiding repetition 1

Figure it out

A How do the speakers in Exercise 1B avoid repeating the same or similar words? Rewrite the underlined parts of the sentences. Then read the grammar chart.

1. Well, she obviously changed careers – a lot of people <u>change careers</u> these days.
2. I hope it works out for her. It <u>worked out</u> for me, but for some people it <u>doesn't work out</u>.
3. She still hasn't gotten any work. I know a lot of graduates who <u>haven't gotten any work</u>.

Auxiliary verbs

Grammar extra
See page 144.

You can avoid repeating words by using auxiliary verbs (e.g., *be, have, do*).

The auxiliary can be in the same tense as the first verb.	*He's obviously enjoying it – as I* **am**. (= am enjoying it) *I think it's a great idea, but my family* **doesn't**. (= doesn't think it's a great idea) *She took a risk, which is what I* **did**, *too.* (= took a risk) *I haven't been abroad. My friends* **haven't** *either.* (= haven't been abroad)
The auxiliary can also be in a different tense	*She obviously changed careers – a lot of people* **do** *these days.* (= change careers) *I hope it works out. It* **did** *for me.* (= worked out)

B Complete the conversations. Use auxiliary verbs. Then practice with a partner.

1. *A* Have you ever taken any risks in life?
   B No, I suppose I haven't really. I went to college, as my brother ________. It was expected, I guess. And I went into dentistry, which is what my dad ________, too. I guess I don't like taking risks. My brother ________, though. He gave up a good career to go into music.
2. *A* So, what's one of the best experiences you've had in life?
   B Well, I guess I've been lucky. I met the perfect guy. And you know, a lot of people ________. And we don't have any financial worries. That's nice. Many couples ________ these days.
3. *A* Have you ever made a decision you regret?
   B Well, let's see. I had the opportunity to go to China on a school trip, but I didn't go. Some of my friends ________, either. But I wish I had. I think they're planning a trip for next year – I hope they ________, anyway. I won't say no next time.
4. *A* Have you traveled much? I mean, where have you been?
   B Well, I haven't traveled much, though all my friends ________. I think it's good to travel, but my parents ________. They worry about me being safe.

About you

C Pair work **Ask and answer the questions in Exercise B. Give your own answers.**

3 Viewpoint My life

Group work **Write your own six-word "memoir" on a piece of paper. Then mix up the papers and take turns reading each one aloud. What can you guess about the writer? Make comparisons with other people. Can you guess who wrote it?**

Loving life. School. Family. Friends. Basketball.

"This person is obviously enjoying life – as I am."

In conversation . . .

You can use *-ly* adverbs to show your attitude to what you say.

Lesson B *Favorite books*

1 Vocabulary in context

A **What are some classic works of literature? Who wrote them? Make a list.**

War and Peace by Leo Tolstoy
The Tale of Genji by Murasaki Shikibu
Iracema by José de Alencar

B CD 1.03 **Listen to people talk about their reading habits. What does each person like to read?**

They say young people don't read literature anymore, so we interviewed people to find out.

Who's your favorite author?
"Well, let's see. . . . I love Isabel Allende's novels. Her best one was . . . oh, wait. **It's on the tip of my tongue**, um, . . . *The Stories of Eva Luna*. I would love to write like her, but I'll never be able to. She's so talented, and she tells these amazing, magical stories. I've read every book she's ever written. I hope she writes a new one soon." *– Michael*

What classic literature have you read?
"I enjoy reading Shakespeare. We had to read his plays in college – well, we were supposed to – but they were too difficult, and I **couldn't make heads or tails of** them. It can be hard to **get your head around** the language. But actually, once you **come to grips** with it, you can see how the plots and characters are still relevant today." *– Maiko*

What's your favorite piece of literature?
"Interestingly enough, it's actually a poem. It's one I **learned by heart** when I was a kid. It's about cats, and I can still recite the whole thing. I can't remember who wrote it, though. As kids we used to love reading poems out loud. I still like to, actually." *– Anita*

What did you read most recently?
"**Off the top of my head**, I can't think of anything. Um, let's think. No, nothing **comes to mind**. I don't read a lot of books, but the ones I like tend to be things like biographies, um, nonfiction, where you learn something and **get something out of** it. I don't **see the point** of reading stories that are just made up." *– Carlos*

Is it important to read classic literature?
"Not really. **It's beyond me** why people think you should read the classics. You don't have to. I know I probably shouldn't read trashy novels, and I try not to, but some of my favorite books are just cheap romance novels by unknown authors. They're the ones that **stick in my mind**." *– Sierra*

What are you reading right now?
"Actually, to tell the truth, I don't read much nowadays. I used to. In fact, I was an avid reader; I used to read a lot, but these days I prefer not to. I listen to the radio more, or podcasts, because with, um, sorry . . . I **lost my train of thought**. Um, yeah." *– Jackson*

Word sort

C **Complete the idioms in the chart. Use the interviews above to help you. Then ask and answer the questions in Exercise B. Use at least six idioms in your answers.**

Understanding	Remembering
I **can't make** heads or tails of it!	**It's** ______ **my tongue.**
It's hard to **get your** ______ **around** it.	We have to **learn it by** ______.
You have to **come to** ______ it.	I don't know **off** ______ **my head.**
You want to **get something** ______ it.	Nothing **comes** ______.
It's ______ **me.**	Sometimes I **lose my** ______.
I don't **see** ______ it.	Her stories ______ **in my mind.**

"I have lots of favorite authors, but one that comes to mind is Paulo Coelho."

Vocabulary notebook
See page 19.

2 **Grammar** Avoiding repetition 2

Figure it out

A How might the people in the interviews continue this first sentence without repeating words? Choose words to delete or change. Then read the grammar chart.

I used to read a lot of trashy novels, but . . .

these days I'm not able to read a lot of trashy novels.
I wasn't supposed to read a lot of trashy novels.
I prefer not to read a lot of trashy novels nowadays.
I haven't read a trashy novel in ages.
the trashy novels I like have gotten too trashy.

Infinitive verb phrases; *one, ones*

Grammar extra See page 145.

You can avoid repeating infinitive verb phrases by using *to* when it is clear what you mean.
I would love to write like her, but I'll never be able ***to****. I mean, I'd like* ***to****, but . . .*
We had to read Shakespeare's plays in college. Well, we were supposed ***to****.*

Notice the negatives with *try* and *prefer*.
I shouldn't read trashy novels, and I try ***not to****, but . . .*
I used to read a lot, but these days I prefer ***not to****.*

You can use *one* or *ones* to avoid repeating countable nouns. Don't use them after *my, your, his,* etc., *some, any,* or *both* unless there is an adjective.
I've read all her books. Her best ***one*** *is . . .*
Of the books I read, the ***ones*** *I like best are nonfiction.*

Common errors

You can omit *one / ones* after *first, second, next, best*, but not after *new, big, small, long,* etc.
I hope she writes a ***new one****.* (NOT . . . ~~*a new*~~.)

B How can you avoid repetition in some of these sentences? Delete words or use *one / ones*. Write *one* or *ones* in parentheses where they are optional.

1. These days I hardly ever pick a book up. Well, I tend not to pick up a book. I'd rather read a magazine.
2. There's a lot of literature I haven't read. I've never read *Moby Dick*, but I'd like to read *Moby Dick* one day.
3. I read plays, especially modern plays. My favorite playwright is Arthur Miller. I've read all his plays. His best play is *The Crucible*. Though you have to *see* it performed to really get something out of it.
4. In elementary school, we had to learn poems by heart. At least we were supposed to learn poems by heart.
5. I read for half an hour in bed every night before I go to sleep. Well, I try to read for half an hour in bed every night.
6. I can't see the point of going into bookstores to buy print books. I tend not to go into bookstores to buy print books. My books are all downloaded onto a tablet. It's cheaper.
7. It's beyond me why people don't listen to audio books more. I love autobiographies, and it's a great way to "read," especially long autobiographies. I always get new audio books if I'm able to get them.
8. I still go to the library to borrow books. The books I get are usually historical novels. They're the best books.
9. I haven't read much classic literature, but I like the work of Jane Austen. Some of her books are also movies, like *Emma* and *Pride and Prejudice*. Both movies are good, but the best movie is *Emma*. That sticks in my mind.

About you

C Pair work **Discuss the sentences in Exercise B. Are any of them true for you?**

Lesson C *I do like it.*

1 Conversation strategy Emphasizing ideas

A **In the last day, how many different things have you read and written? Make two lists.**

"I read a friend's blog. I wrote a comment on my friend's social network page."

B CD 1.04 **Listen. What views are mentioned about reading and writing today?**

Professor Not long ago, they were predicting that because of the increase in phone and computer use, people would stop reading and writing. But we haven't. In fact, we're reading and writing more than we did. So, are there implications of this for literature? And if so, what?

Yolanda Yes, well, it does seem that with social media everybody's writing something these days, like blogs and check-ins and status updates. I know I am.

Elena Which is a good thing. I mean, I do like the fact that anyone can write a blog. It makes writing, well, . . . more democratic somehow.

Professor I do think, though, that it gives the impression that anybody can be a writer. But doesn't it take talent to be a good writer? And if not, then does that mean anything goes?

Tariq Yes, nowadays anyone can publish a novel online, but how do you know if it's any good? How do we evaluate it?

Yolanda Do you need to, though? I think the real problem is with nonfiction. I mean, how do you determine what information you read on the Internet is accurate and reliable?

Professor Yes, indeed. That's just as important, if not more important.

C **Notice** how the speakers add a stressed auxiliary verb (*do, does*) before a main verb to add emphasis to what they say. Find more examples in the conversation.

It does seem that everyone's writing something these days.

In conversation . . .

The most common phrases with ***I do*** are: *I do think, I do like, I do know, I do want, I do enjoy, I do believe, I do feel, I do agree.*

D CD 1.05 **Read the conversations. Add the auxiliary verbs *do* or *does* to add emphasis where possible, and make any other necessary changes. Then listen and check.**

1. *A* The problem with many of the blogs you read is that they're very poorly written.
   B Yeah. I think it's hard to find ones that are well written. Some have good content, though.
2. *A* You know what I hate? Microblogs. I feel they're a waste of time and not worth reading.
   B Well, I follow some celebrities. I enjoy reading their thoughts on life.
3. *A* I believe that people are much less afraid of writing now. I know I am. It used to be so hard to get your work published, but not anymore. The Internet really makes a difference.
   B But it seems like that's the problem. Anyone can get their work out there.
4. *A* It's interesting how new kinds of writing have come about in recent years. Like those cell phone novels that started in Japan. It makes you wonder why they became so popular.
   B Yeah. It seems unlikely that people would want to read books on a cell phone.

About you

E Pair work **Discuss the conversations in Exercise D. Do you agree with the views presented? What other views do you have about each topic?**

2 Strategy plus *If so, if not*

CD 1.06 You can use ***if so***, especially in formal speaking. It means "if the answer is 'yes'" or "if this is true."

Are there any implications of this for literature? And **if so**, what?

If not means "if the answer is 'no'" or "if this is not true."

*And **if not**, then does that mean anything goes?*

You can also use ***if not*** to restate something with more emphasis.

*That's just as important, **if not** more important.*

In conversation . . .

If not is more frequent.

If not ■■■■■■■■

If so ■

A CD 1.07 **Listen to five students' concerns about researching information online. Number the professor's responses 1–5.**

a. ☐ Well, you'll need to develop the skill of deciding what's relevant. If not, you'll waste a lot of time.
b. ☐ Well, if so, don't use it. You should only use trusted sources for your essays.
c. ☐ That could be dangerous. You need to consult a professional. If not, you could damage your health.
d. ☐ If so, you need to write that in your paper and describe the different outcomes of each study.
e. ☐ It is, and they could fail if they're found out; plagiarism is wrong, if not dishonest.

About you

B Pair work **Discuss the problems. Do you have similar ones? How do you solve them?**

3 Listening and strategies The blogosphere

A CD 1.08 **Guess the missing words and numbers on the slide. Then listen to part of a presentation. Write a word or number in each space.**

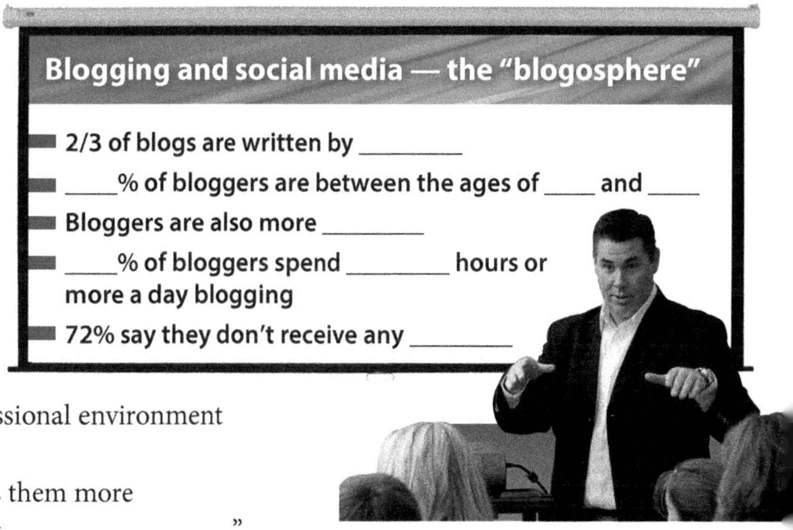

B CD 1.09 **Listen to the next part of the presentation. Complete the notes on the reasons for blogging.**

1. "Bloggers' main motivation for writing blogs does appear to be more about ________________."
2. ". . . the motivation to blog in a professional environment does seem to be ________________."
3. "Bloggers do say that blogging makes them more committed to, if not passionate about, ________________."
4. "There is a sense that bloggers are blogging because they really do ________________."
5. ". . . those people who do derive supplementary income from their blog sites tend to ________________."

About you

C Pair work **Discuss the questions.**

- Do you read or write blogs?
- Are you more likely to now?
- Did the presentation change your views about blogging?
- Did it give you any new information?

A Well, to be honest, I don't read many blogs, but it does seem that they could be interesting.
B Yes. I do think that they might be a useful way of promoting yourself at work, for example.

Speaking naturally
See page 138.

Lesson D *Poetry*

1 Reading

A Prepare Do you or your friends enjoy reading poetry? Who are some of the famous poets you know of? Make a list.

"Octavio Paz is a well-known poet here."

B Read for main ideas Read the article and the extracts from some poems. What kinds of poetry does it refer to? What are the features of each type?

A brief history of *poetry*

1 In the Museum of the Ancient Orient in Istanbul, Turkey, there is a small tablet with ancient Sumerian script on it. Few people have been able to read it, but Turkish historian and archaeologist Muazzez İlmiye Çiğ believed that the words on the tablet are those of a lover from 4,000 years ago and that it is the oldest love poem ever found.

2 Of course, love has been one of the enduring themes of poetry for centuries. Additionally, in pre-literate society, poetry was often used as a means of keeping oral history alive, for storytelling, or simply as a way of recording family history or law, for example. Indeed, these societies had no other means of registering important events or cultural information, and reciting poetry was a way to pass what they held dear from generation to generation.

3 Poetry was also valued in religion as a way of remembering teachings and prophecies. Many of the world's sacred scriptures are written in poetic verse. Early agrarian societies used poetry in rituals to encourage a good harvest, while early Chinese poetry evolved from folk songs.

4 One of the earliest known Western poems is Homer's *The Iliad*, written in the eighth century BCE. It is typical of an epic poem and consists of 15,000 lines in a strict rhythmic structure. It tells of the war between the Acheans and Trojans and talks of gods and heroes like Achilles and Patroclus. With themes of war and fate, it is believed that *The Iliad* was learned by heart and repeated as part of passing on cultural values and educational messages.

An extract from *The Iliad*

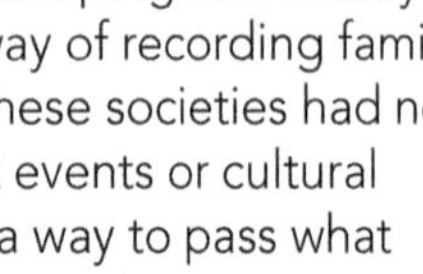

Patroclus asks his friend Achilles for permission to join the battle, which Achilles has left.

"Give me your armor to put on your shoulders;
The Trojans might suppose I was you,
Hold back, and give the Acheans' sons a breather,
For breathing spells in war are very few.
Then, with a shout, fresh men might easily
Turn tired men from the ships toward the city."

5 During the European Renaissance, (late 15th to early 17th century), a poetic form that became popular was the sonnet. This has only 14 lines of verse. William Shakespeare, who was one of the many Renaissance poets, composed 154 of them.

An extract from Shakespeare's Sonnet 18

Shakespeare is praising the lasting beauty of a woman.

Shall I compare thee to a summer's day?
Thou art more lovely and more temperate:
Rough winds do shake the darling buds of May,
And summer's lease hath all too short a date:

6 In other cultures, there are different forms of traditional poetry. Japanese *haiku* is structured with 17 syllables in a 5-7-5-syllable pattern. Haiku often describes nature and communicates an abstract idea or a feeling in a moment in time. One eighteenth-century master *haiku* poet – Kobayashi Issa – wrote about his sadness on the death of his third child and then his wife.

Haiku by Kobayashi Issa

Ikinokori
ikinokoritaru
samusa kana.

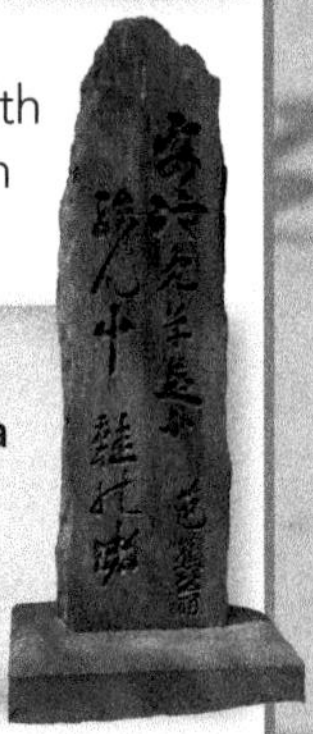

7 While the forms of poetry have changed over time, it has generally retained a style and rhythm that make it different from other forms of writing such as novels, essays, letters, or articles. Nevertheless, one of the continuing debates centers around the issue of "What is poetry?" – a debate that still goes on with the rise of rap culture in the United States. Some see rap as the return of poetry as a performance art – poetry that should be heard rather than read – while critics say that rap should not be considered as poetry at all because it does not use "correct" English. Regardless of the ongoing debate, many rappers do consider themselves as poets. Certainly, the topics of rap songs are those of love, war, life, and death – something that hasn't changed since poetry first established itself as an art form.

Reading tip

In the last sentence or paragraph, writers often return to the theme raised at the start of the piece.

C Read for main ideas **Find the ideas below in the article. Write the paragraph number.**

Which paragraph mentions the following?	Paragraph
1. the belief that poetry could improve crop yields	________
2. how poetry was used to register births and family relationships	________
3. the controversy surrounding a definition of what poetry actually is	________
4. how certain poetic forms express ideas that are difficult to define	________
5. the notion of poets as teachers	________
6. an example of how romantic poetry has existed for thousands of years	________
7. the spiritual applications of poetry	________

2 Focus on vocabulary Synonyms

Tip

Writers use synonyms to avoid repeating the same word. The more synonyms you know, the easier a text is to understand.

A **In each question, circle the two words in bold that are similar in meaning. Use the article to help you. Paragraph numbers are given in parentheses.**

1. What are some of the **abstract (6)** / **enduring (2)** / **lasting (5)** themes of poetry?
2. Why was poetry **retained (7)** / **held dear (2)** / **valued (3)** in early societies?
3. In early societies, poetry was used for **recording (2)** / **consisting of (4)** / **registering (2)** what?
4. What famous poem describes a **war (4)** / **values (4)** / **battle (4)**?
5. Who **wrote (6)** / **evolved (3)** / **composed (5)** sonnets?
6. Which cultures used poetry as a **way (3)** / **fate (4)** / **means (2)** of educating audiences?
7. What is the nature of the **ongoing (7)** / **continuing (7)** / **communicating (6)** debate about rap?
8. Do you have a favorite **verse (3)** / **poem (1)** / **prophecy (3)**?

B Pair work **Discuss the questions in Exercise A. Use the article to help you. Also add your own ideas and views.**

3 Listening My interpretation is . . .

A CD 1.10 **Read and listen to the poem. Who is the poet talking about?**

PRIME by Amy Lowell

Your voice is like bells
over roofs at dawn

When a bird flies

And the sky changes to a
fresher color.

Speak, speak, Beloved.

Say little things

For my ears to catch

And run with them to
my heart.

B CD 1.11 **Listen to one person's interpretation of the poem. How does the person answer these questions?**

1. What do you think of the poem? She thinks . . .
2. What image does it bring to mind?
3. How do you think the poet feels?
4. How does it make you feel?

About you

C Pair work **Discuss the questions in Exercise B. Do you agree?**

Writing *A short yet powerful novel . . .*

In this lesson, you . . .

- write a book review.
- link adjectives.
- avoid errors with *yet*.

Task **Write a review of a book.**

Choose a book that you have enjoyed and write a review of it for the "Book Club" section of a magazine.

A Look at a model **Look at the review of a novel. What does the writer think of the novel? Underline adjectives that are linked together.**

A short yet powerful novel, John Steinbeck's *Of Mice and Men* is set in California during the Depression of the 1930s. It tells the story of the friendship of two ranch workers and their hopes and dreams. Lennie, a physically large but gentle man of limited intelligence, and George, his tough yet compassionate and caring friend, share a dream that will be difficult, if not impossible, to fulfill: owning a piece of land.

Throughout the novel, Steinbeck creates an atmosphere that is dark and menacing. It is clear from the start that this is a story that is not going to have a happy ending. Its dramatic, though not entirely unexpected, ending leaves the reader feeling sad but perhaps hopeful that the values of friendship and trust remain stronger than the desperate reality that George and Lennie inhabit.

Brilliantly written, *Of Mice and Men* is compelling, if at times depressing, with themes that are as relevant today as they were then. It is a magnificent work of fiction.

B Focus on language **Read the chart. Then choose the best options to complete the sentences below. Sometimes all are correct.**

Linking adjectives in writing

You can link two related or compatible adjectives with *and* or use a comma before a noun.
George is a ***compassionate and caring*** *friend.* OR *George is a* ***compassionate, caring*** *friend.*

Use *but, yet,* or *though* to link adjectives with a contrasting meaning. *If* can introduce a negative idea.
Lennie is a physically ***large but gentle*** *man . . .*
A ***short yet powerful*** *novel, . . .*
Its ***dramatic, though not unexpected****, ending . . .*
It is ***compelling, if*** *at times* ***depressing****.*

You can use *if not* or *(or) even* to add a stronger adjective.
Their dream will be ***difficult, if not / (or) even impossible****, to fulfill.*

Common errors

Use *yet* in academic writing. Use *but* in most other cases.
I enjoyed the book, ***but*** *it was a little long.* (NOT . . . ~~*yet it was*~~ . . .)

1. It is an engaging **and / , / but** thought-provoking story about two men.
2. The novel has several scenes that are unbearably tense **and / , / , if not** disturbing.
3. The lives of the characters are hard, **if not / even / though** desperate.
4. Their dreams are understandable **yet / but / though / if** ultimately unrealistic.
5. The writing is simple **yet / but / ,** deeply symbolic.
6. The ending is moving, **if not / even / but** poignant, with an act that is compassionate, **even / though / if** brutal.

C Write and check **Write a short review of a book. Exchange reviews with your classmates.**

Writing a book review

Describe the setting, plot, characters, and themes. Evaluate the book. Write a recommendation.

Vocabulary notebook *Heads or tails*

Learning tip Situations

When you learn an idiom, it's useful to think of a situation when you can use it. Write down the situation and then a sentence using the idiom.

You're trying to follow some instructions to put together a bookshelf.
"I can't make heads or tails of these instructions."

A Match the situations with the expressions. Write the letters a–f.

1. You're taking a class, but you're not sure you're learning anything. ____
2. Someone has just unfriended you on your social networking site – you have no idea why. ____
3. You're trying to remember the name of the author of a book you've just read. ____
4. You have to give a short presentation in class without using any notes. ____
5. You're telling someone a story, but you get distracted. ____
6. You're telling someone about something memorable that happened to you when you were little. ____

a. ***It's beyond me*** *why he did that.*
b. *I have to* ***learn it by heart.***
c. *Sorry. I* ***lost my train of thought.***
d. *I hope I* ***get something out of*** *this.*
e. *That really* ***sticks in my mind.***
f. ***It's on the tip of my tongue.***

B Look at these idioms. Think of a situation when you might use each idiom. Write the situations.

1. ______________________ "It's hard to get your head around."
2. ______________________ "I can't come to grips with it."
3. ______________________ "I really don't see the point of it."
4. ______________________ "Gosh, I don't know off the top of my head."
5. ______________________ "Well, nothing really comes to mind."

C Word builder Find the meanings of these idioms. Then write a situation for each one.

1. jog your memory
2. go in one ear and out the other
3. ring a bell
4. get the message
5. miss the point
6. it's a no-brainer

D Focus on vocabulary Write one word from the box that has a similar meaning to the words in bold. Then write answers to the questions. **Refer to Exercise 2A on page 17 to help you.**

battle	continuing	composed	lasting
means of	register	value	verse

1. What is something that you **hold dear**?
2. What's one of your **enduring** memories from childhood?
3. What information do you have to **record** on a birth certificate?
4. What famous **war** have you learned about in history?
5. When was the last time you **wrote** a poem?
6. What's the best **way of** recording your family history?
7. Do you have any **ongoing** ambitions?
8. Have you ever learned a **poem** by heart?

Unit 2

Technology

In Unit 2, you . . .

- talk about technology and its impact.
- add information to nouns.
- use conjunctions such as *both . . . and . . .* and *neither . . . nor . . .*
- signal expectations with adverbs like *presumably* and *ironically.*
- use *can't / couldn't possibly* to say what is impossible.

Lesson A *How private is "private"?*

1 Grammar in context

A How private do you consider these things to be? What else do you consider as private?

- your cell phone number
- your date of birth
- your marital status
- your mailing address
- favorite websites
- your photographs

B CD 1.12 **Listen to a seminar. What invasions of privacy do the students mention?**

Professor: In the college debate next week, the subject to be discussed is changing attitudes toward privacy. Do you think privacy has a different meaning nowadays?

Gert: Yes, definitely. I mean, people put pictures online and share intimate details with hundreds of so-called friends on social networks. You can watch videos of absolutely anything, you know, people brushing their teeth – all kinds of things that were once considered private.

Ricard: Right. And every few minutes, they post updates saying what they're doing. "The cat just bit me," or "Gonna wash my hair." We don't need to know things like that.

Lorraine: True. You can get to know more about people on the other side of the world than about someone next door or the guy upstairs. But I guess it's pretty harmless.

Gert: Maybe, but what about real invasions of privacy? Like online stores bombard you with ads offering personal recommendations because they know what you've searched for. And applications programmed to monitor your email, then on your screen you get those pop-up ads based on what you've just written? They're the ones I find creepy.

Lorraine: Well, you can just ignore ads. What worries me is the information demanded from you if you just want a username for a website – sometimes they want your mailing address, cell phone number, date of birth . . . everything. There must be a lot of people happy to give away all this information, but they have no idea of how it'll be used. They get taken in by websites eager to make money by selling their databases to other companies.

Professor: Privacy is not an easy concept to define. So, let's see if we can come up with a definition of privacy.

C Pair work **Discuss the questions.**

1. What do you think Gert means by "so-called friends"?
2. What is Lorraine referring to when she says "But I guess it's pretty harmless"?
3. Why do you think Gert uses the word *bombard*?
4. Why are some websites a cause for concern, in Lorraine's opinion?
5. Which of the students' views do you agree with?

2 Grammar Adding information to nouns

Figure it out

A Write how the students say these things without relative clauses. Then read the chart.

1. the guy who lives upstairs
2. websites that are eager to make money
3. ads that offer personal recommendations
4. pop-up ads that are based on what you've just written

Noun phrases

Grammar extra See page 146.

You can add information to nouns with different types of expressions instead of using a relative clause.

An adverb or adverbial phrase	*the guy* ***upstairs*** (= who lives upstairs), *someone* ***next door***
A prepositional phrase	*people* ***on the other side of the world***
An adjective phrase	*people* ***happy to give away this information***
An active infinitive	*an easy concept* ***to define***
A passive infinitive has a future meaning	*the subject* ***to be discussed***
A present participle (*-ing* form)	*ads* ***offering personal recommendations***
A past participle has a passive meaning	*applications* ***programmed to monitor your messages***

B CD 1.13 **Rewrite the comments. Replace the underlined words with the type of phrase given. Do you agree with the comments? Discuss with a partner.**

1. The invasion of privacy is an important matter that we should discuss. (active infinitive) I mean, how to protect our privacy is an issue that should be taken seriously. (passive infinitive) And anyone who is willing to part with personal information is just taking a risk. (adjective phrase)
2. I hate it when online stores monitor the items that you have put in your basket and then bombard you with emails that offer you discounts on those same things. (prepositional phrase, present participle) I delete all emails that are sent by shopping websites on principle. (past participle)
3. It's useful that they send advertisements that they target at you personally. (past participle) Sometimes you get discount coupons that are for things you really need. (prepositional phrase)
4. Giving your phone number in stores to get a refund is nothing that we should worry about. (active infinitive) The thing we should watch is when they want your fingerprints. (active infinitive)
5. Friends who share your personal details with strangers – that's one of the potential dangers that exist in social networking. (present participle, prepositional phrase) For example, I know far too much about the person in the apartment that is downstairs. (adverb)

3 Listening and speaking Privacy or convenience?

A When do people have to give their fingerprints? Is it a reasonable request?

B CD 1.14 **Listen to Mark tell Mary about a trip to a theme park. Are the sentences true (T) or false (F)? Correct the false information.**

1. Mark knew beforehand that he would have to give his fingerprint. ____
2. The man behind Mark in the line agreed with Mark's point of view. ____
3. Mary thinks the theme park knows that people will object. ____
4. Mary would rather be inconvenienced than give her personal information. ____
5. Mark's wife thought it was a convenient way of opening the lockers. ____

About you

C Pair work **What do you think of Mark's story? What would you have done in his position?**

Speaking naturally See page 138.

Lesson B *A smarter home*

1 Vocabulary in context

A What items of technology do most people have in their homes? Make a list.

B CD 1.15 **Read the article. Are any of the items of technology from your list mentioned?**

Who's smarter, YOU or the BUILDING?

In many parts of the world, **labor-saving** appliances such as dishwashers and vacuum cleaners are regarded neither as remarkable objects nor as luxuries. In others, both **solar-powered** and **wind-powered** energy supplement the regular electricity supply, so people can enjoy **energy-efficient** or even **carbon-neutral, air-conditioned** comfort. Many homes boast not only **high-speed** Internet connections but also **high-tech** streaming entertainment systems. It might seem as if there is nothing left to invent nor any domestic task that cannot be automated. Homes are getting smarter, and in the not-too-distant future, the so-called ultra-modern home will be available to all. Here's how your day might look very soon.

7:00 a.m. Your bedside alarm decides when to wake you by checking the schedule downloaded from your computer. It plays either easy-listening music or bird song (or any sound of your choice), getting louder as the lights fade up to just the right level. The blinds open to reveal sparkling **self-cleaning** windows. Meanwhile, in your state-of-the-art kitchen, a **custom-built** robot is preparing your breakfast as you head for the **climate-controlled** shower room. A touch-screen panel in the mirror either reads your messages to you or gives you the traffic and weather reports you'll need for the day.

6:30 p.m. You say, "I'm home" as you get back from work. The hallway lights go on, and the aroma of a **home-cooked** meal wafts out of the kitchen. You enter the kitchen; the lights go on, and off in the hallway. The lifelike robot greets you with a **human-like** "Hello" and serves dinner.

10:30 p.m. The **computer-controlled** system takes over. It not only powers down the lights and the heating, but it also locks down the house and activates the security system. Everything is going well until you make a **last-minute** decision to go out to a late movie. Now . . . what was that top-secret, voice-activated code for overriding the whole smart operating system to unlock the front door?

About you

C Pair work **Discuss the questions.**

1. Which items of technology in the article would you like to have? Why?
2. Which items do you think will become common in the next 10 to 15 years?
3. Are there any items that you think are frivolous or not particularly useful?

Word sort

D Find compound adjectives in the article to complete the chart. Add seven more from the article. Then use the adjectives to describe technology that you use or know about.

climate -controlled	custom-	1.	5.
-efficient	home-	2.	6.
-like	high-	3.	7.
-powered	labor-	4.	
air-	last-		
carbon-	self-		

"We have a climate-controlled section in the refrigerator for fresh produce."

Vocabulary notebook

See page 29.

2 Grammar Combining ideas

Figure it out

A Use the article to help you rewrite these sentences. Then read the grammar chart.

1. Solar-powered and wind-powered energy supplement the regular electricity supply.
2. Dishwashers are not regarded as remarkable objects or luxuries.
3. It gradually powers down the lights, and it activates the security system.

either . . . or, both . . . and, neither . . . nor, not only . . . but also

Grammar extra See page 147.

You can use these conjunctions to combine two phrases or clauses in one clause or one sentence.

Use *either . . . or . . .* to list two alternatives.	*It plays **either** easy-listening music **or** birdsong.* *It **either** reads your messages **or** gives you a traffic report.*
Use *both . . . and . . .* to combine two phrases or clauses in an affirmative context.	***Both** solar-powered **and** wind-powered energy supplement the regular electricity supply.*
Use *neither . . . nor . . .* to combine two phrases or clauses in a negative context.	*Dishwashers and vacuum cleaners are regarded **neither** as remarkable objects **nor** as luxuries.*
Use *not only . . . but also . . .* to combine two phrases or clauses in a more emphatic way.	*Many homes boast **not only** high-speed Internet connections **but also** high-tech entertainment systems.*

Common errors

Use *both . . . and . . .* to emphasize that there are two people or things.
Use *either . . . or . . .* when there is a choice of alternatives.
*Technology improves **both** our efficiency **and** our quality of life.*
(NOT . . . ~~*improves either . . . or*~~ . . .)

B Rewrite the comments using the conjunctions given. You may have to change the form or order of the words, or leave some words out. Then practice with a partner.

1. *A* You know what I don't like? High-tech gadgets with all those functions that you don't want or use. (neither . . . nor) Like my alarm clock tells the time and gives the temperature outside. (not only . . . but also)
   B It's like my cell phone. I don't open the calendar, and I don't use the voice-activated calling. (neither . . . nor)
2. *A* You know, chores were much harder for our grandparents' generation. I mean, my grandmother washed everything by hand, and she hung it out to dry. (not only . . . but also)
   B Well, they didn't have the luxury or the convenience of all our labor-saving devices. (neither . . . nor)
3. *A* Imagine running your home from your laptop. You could control the heating system, the lights. (both . . . and) Well, everything, really. Then if you forgot to turn off the stove or the coffee pot, you could just do it when you got to work. (either . . . or)
   B It'd be handy, too, on vacation. I mean, you could check on your house and you could water your plants. (not only . . . but also)
4. *A* I'd love a robot that can cook or clean. (either . . . or) I think chores are boring and a waste of time. (both . . . and)
   B Me too. My friend bought one of those robot vacuum cleaners. It saved her time and did a better job than she did. (not only . . . but also)

About you

C Pair work **What do you think about the views above? Discuss your ideas. Do you agree?**

Lesson C *Invariably, it's more efficient.*

1 Conversation strategy Signaling expectations

A **Do you think you're good at multitasking? What two things can you do at the same time?**

B CD 1.16 **Listen. What does the research that Lucia read say about multitasking?**

Rashad All these people with headphones on – working, emailing, messaging . . . I couldn't possibly do that.

Lucia Me neither.

Rashad I mean, multitasking is supposedly an essential skill these days, and theoretically, you can pack 12 hours into an 8-hour day, but I'm skeptical. You can't possibly concentrate on more than one thing.

Lucia Well, I was reading about this recently, and evidently, if you're multitasking, you're either doing things badly or not at all.

Rashad So there's been research on this, presumably?

Lucia Yeah. Apparently, they gave people these tasks to do and found that "high multitaskers" weren't just slower; they had poor memories and couldn't switch tasks easily, either. So being able to multitask is really a myth and might even be harmful.

Rashad Sounds like there's a lot to be said for doing one thing at a time.

Lucia Well, it's almost invariably more efficient. And ironically, the people who said they were bad at multitasking performed better than those who said they were good at it, and vice versa.

Rashad Maybe I'd be better at it than I thought, then.

C **Notice** how Rashad and Lucia use adverbs to signal what they predict, expect, or assume to be true. Find the examples they use in the conversation.

Adverbs can express what you . . .
predict: ***predictably, inevitably, invariably***
expect: ***presumably, supposedly;*** **don't expect:** ***ironically***
assume to be true: ***evidently, apparently, supposedly***
think is possible (in theory): ***potentially, theoretically***
think is ideal: ***ideally***

D **Rewrite the sentences, replacing the underlined words with the adverb form of the word in bold. Then discuss the information with a partner. Do you agree?**

Mothers supposedly spend a lot more time . . .

1. Mothers are **supposed** to spend a lot more time multitasking than fathers, or so people say. The **invariable** belief is that they're making dinner and helping the kids with homework.
2. There is the **potential** that multitasking for a period of time can overload the brain and cause stress. It **appears** that it's harmful to the brain.
3. There is **evidence** that workers distracted by phone calls and email suffer a drop in IQ. The **ideal** thing is you should avoid distractions. The **potential** is it's like losing a night's sleep.
4. Some people think multitasking makes them more productive, which is **ironic**. You have to **presume** that they haven't read the research about its effect on your brain.
5. In **theory**, it's possible for multitasking to be addictive. The **invariable** habit of high multitaskers is to place a high value on new information. They switch from emails to texts to calls because it's exciting to them, which is **inevitable**.

2 Strategy plus *can't possibly . . .*

CD 1.17 You can use ***can't possibly*** or ***couldn't possibly*** to emphasize that something is impossible.

A CD 1.18 **Listen. Five people talk about multitasking. Number the summaries of their views 1–5.**

☐ All young people do it.
☐ You get less work done.
☐ It's dangerous while driving.
☐ It affects your concentration.
☐ It's actually pretty easy.

B CD 1.19 **Read the responses below. Then listen again and number the responses 1–5.**

_____ Right. You couldn't possibly say that multitasking is a good skill to have, then.
_____ Yeah, it can't possibly be that hard to do two simple everyday tasks at the same time.
_____ Right. You can't possibly concentrate on driving if you're on the phone.
_____ I know. I mean, you can't possibly expect them to do anything different.
_____ Exactly. But you can't possibly avoid phone calls and things, even if you work at home.

About you **C** CD 1.20 **Listen again. Write your own responses. Then compare with a partner.**

3 Listening and strategies How do you multitask?

A CD 1.21 **Listen to three conversations. Write answers for each item below.**

1. Write the job each multitasker has.
2. Write three tasks each multitasker does at the same time.
3. Write the mistake each multitasker admits to.

B CD 1.22 **Listen again to some of the things the speakers say. Complete the comments below with expressions from the box. There are two extra expressions.**

can't possibly	couldn't possibly	inevitably	invariably	ironically	potentially	presumably

1. You _______________ expect people to do three or four things at the same time and do each thing properly.
2. _______________, I end up making mistakes when I try to do more than one thing at once. It's usually better to take your time.
3. That's what drives me crazy – trying to have a conversation with someone and they're checking messages on their phone. _______________, I just make an excuse and leave.
4. I don't know about you, but I _______________ just sit and watch a TV show. I have to do other stuff at the same time.
5. I can see you can listen to music and study – it helps you concentrate, _______________. I mean, that kind of multitasking seems fine.

About you **C** Pair work **Do you agree with the comments above? Discuss with a partner.**

A Actually, I agree. You can't possibly expect people to do three or four things at the same time and do each thing properly.
B Oh, I totally agree. I mean, invariably you end up making a mistake with something.

Lesson D *Technology adoptions*

1 Reading

A Prepare **When new gadgets come onto the market, how many people in the class: a. buy them immediately? b. wait and see what other people say about them? c. never buy them? Take a class vote.**

B Read for main ideas **Read the article to see if your class fits the model in the diagram. Complete the labels in the diagram with terms and percentages in the article to help you find out.**

As technology changes, so do adoption lifecycles

1 For decades now, conventional marketing wisdom about product adoption cycles has been based on a model first described in the 1950s. The Adoption Process model (also known as the Diffusion of Innovation) illustrates how consumers purchase new products and services (see Rogers, 2003*). It categorizes consumers according to their behavior as early adopters at one end of the cycle and laggards at the other.

2 Until recently, cutting-edge technologies were mainly used by a minority group of "innovators," who accounted for approximately 2 percent of consumers. These were the enthusiasts that tried out every new gadget on the market. They were also the ones who found any bugs or problems in the products, gave honest feedback, and became loyal users. The next group of customers were the more cautious "early adopters," who represented 13.5 percent of consumers. Then came the majority of mainstream consumers, who are described as "early majority" and "late majority" consumers, each group representing 34 percent of the total market. They viewed new technology with more caution. Typically, they waited until a new piece of technology was truly tried and tested and until the price had been considerably reduced. It invariably took several years for this to happen, and at this point, when the majority of consumers had purchased a product, it was said that it had truly penetrated the market and become a mainstream "must-have" item. The remaining 16 percent of consumers are labeled "laggards" – that is, those who are either very late adopters or who never buy high-tech products.

3 However, some researchers are beginning to find that these typical adoption patterns are becoming less relevant in today's marketplace and that mainstream consumers are *all* becoming early adopters. The length of time it takes for a new technology to enter the mainstream market is also shortening. When tablets hit the market in 2010, it was the fastest uptake of any device ever. It was faster than the spread of laptops and faster than the penetration of smart phones. Over 15 million tablets were sold in the first nine months after the initial release – a phenomenal rate by any standards.

4 Furthermore, in the past, advanced technologies often first appeared in the workplace and then migrated into the domestic setting as recreational products. That is no longer the case, and it is increasingly the general domestic consumer who is driving what is used in the workplace, as employees show up at work with their new "toys" and expect to be able to use them. Authors of one study point out that the average family is now instrumental in driving recent technology adoptions. Having the latest technology is one way to catalog your children growing up and share it with other family members. Over 85 percent of families with children have cell phones, and they are more likely to have both music and video playback features on their phones.

Technology Adoption Life Cycle

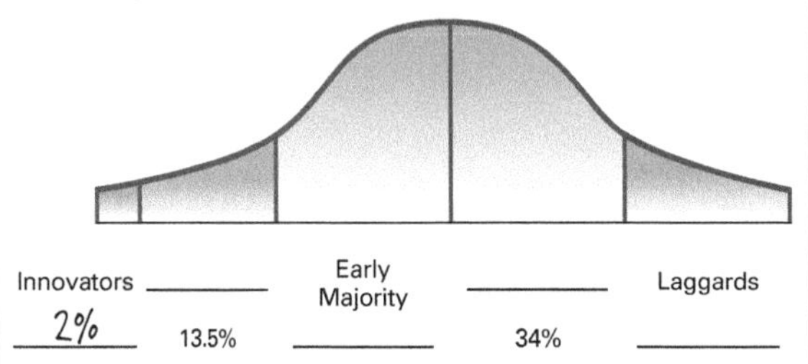

5 Perhaps part of the reason for the change in how technologies are adopted is that the millennial generation is now a much larger segment of the consumer population. Millennials, that is, children born in the 1980s, grew up with media and digital technologies. Generation Z kids born in the 1990s are even more connected and net-savvy and are often known as "digital-natives." In the near future, they will become the majority of the consumer population, and the only logical assumption is that the technology lifecycle as described in traditional models may well be obsolete and in need of radical revision.

*Rogers, E.M. 2003. *Diffusion of Innovations* (5th Edition). New York: Free Press.

Reading tip

Writers sometimes explain a term using *that is, or,* parentheses ( ), or a dash – . ***Millennials, that is,** children born in the 1980s* , . . .

C Check your understanding **Find words in the article with a similar meaning to the words in bold below. Use those words to answer the questions.**

1. What does the product adoption cycle **show**? (para. 1) It illustrates . . .
2. The model **groups** or **classifies** consumers into five types. What are they? (para. 1)
3. When did the majority of consumers typically **buy** a product? (para. 1)
4. What percentage of consumers does the "early adopter" group **represent**? (para. 2)
5. What product **got into** the market more quickly than any other? (para. 2)
6. What trends are marketers now noticing after the **first launch** of a product? (para. 3)
7. What is driving technology adoptions: the workplace or **home** use? (para. 4)
8. What influence are younger people having as a **section** of the consumer population? (para. 5)

D React Pair work **Ask and answer the questions in Exercise C. Do you recognize the trends described in the article?**

2 Focus on vocabulary Suffixes

Study tip

Learn suffixes like *-al / -ical* for adjectives and *-tion / -sion* for nouns. In reading, they can help you understand new words. In writing, using different word forms helps you avoid repetition.

A **In this summary of the article, complete the second sentences with a form of the bold words in the first sentences.The words can all be found in the article**

1. Technology companies love to **innovate** and hope that consumers will **adopt** their products quickly. However, consumers vary in their approach to innovation ______ and their ______ of new technology.
2. Consumers used to be more **cautious**. Their ______ was due to the high price of gadgets.
3. Tablets immediately **penetrated** the market and became a **phenomenon**. Such a rapid ______ of the market was truly ______.
4. New gadgets used to be for work, not **recreation**. Once they became ______, the market grew.
5. The children who reached adulthood at the **millennium** are now consumers. This ______ generation is less conservative and more net-savvy than older generations.
6. We can no longer **assume** that Bourne's model is still relevant. Our ______ have to change.
7. The market has changed **radically**, and experts are **revising** their theories. Bourne's model therefore needs a ______ ______.

B Pair work **Take turns using the words in Exercise A to discuss your observations about how people buy and use technology.**

3 Viewpoint What type of consumer are you?

Group work **Discuss the questions.**

- How would you describe yourself as a technology consumer? Are you an early adopter? A laggard?
- How about other types of purchases? Do you have the same approach?
- What new technologies have recently been released into the market? Which ones interest you?
- Describe someone you know – anyone who's a different consumer type from you with regard to technology. What do you think of that approach?
- What differences, if any, do you see between the generations and their approach to buying technology?

"Well, let's see, I suppose you could say that I'm in the late majority of consumers. I tend to wait . . ."

In conversation . . .

If you need time to think, you can say *Let's see* or *Let me think*.

Writing *The bar graph illustrates . . .*

In this lesson, you . . .

- describe graphs, charts, and tables.
- describe and compare statistics.
- avoid errors with *as can be seen, etc.*

Task Write a report about Internet use.

Write a report for a business class or your employer about Internet use. Use graphs, charts, or tables in your report.

A Look at a model **Look at the graph and complete the paragraph.**

The bar graph illustrates the percentage of the population who were Internet users in each geographic region in ________. As can be seen in the graph, North America accounted for the highest percentage of Internet users in comparison with other regions, at ________ %, followed by ________ at 67.8%. In comparison, the region with the lowest percentage was ________, which represents ________ % of Internet users.

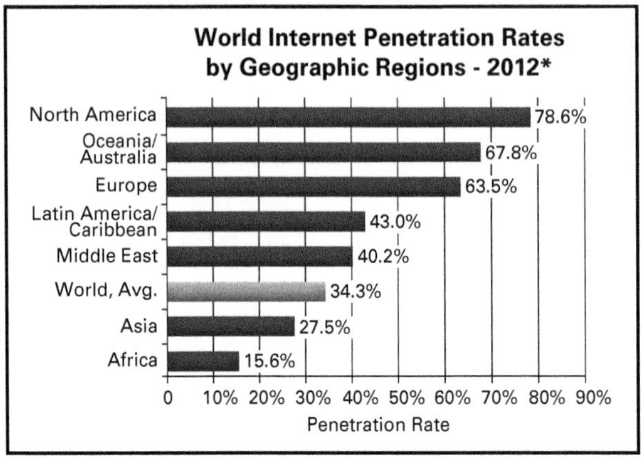

B Focus on language **Read the chart. Then underline the expressions for describing and comparing in the paragraph in Exercise A.**

Describing and comparing information in graphs

The graph shows / illustrates . . . ***As can be seen*** *in the graph . . .* ***. . . as shown*** *in the table.*
In 2012, Internet users ***accounted for / represented*** *32.7 percent of the world population.*
North America had a high percentage of users ***in comparison to / compared*** *to Africa.*
In comparison / contrast, *Africa had the lowest percentage of Internet users.*

Common errors

Do not add *it* to the expressions *as can be seen, as is shown.*
As can be seen *in the pie chart, most Internet users live in Asia.*
(NOT *As ~~it~~ can be seen in the pie chart, . . .*)

C Write and check **Write a report on Internet use, using the information from the graph in Exercise A and the pie chart below. Then check for errors.**

The pie chart shows the percentage of Internet users by world region. As can be seen in the chart, the highest percentage of users are in Asia. They account for 44.8% of the world's users. . . .

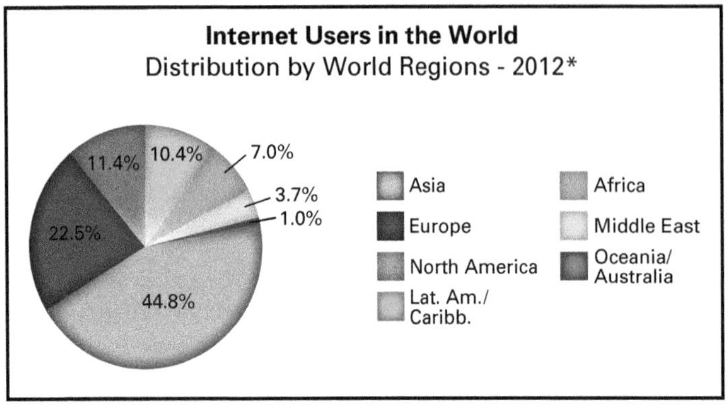

*Source: Adapted from Internet World Stats - www.internetworldstats.com/stats.htm. Penetration Rates are based on a world population of 7,012,519,841 and 2,405,510,175 estimated Internet users on June 30, 2012. Copyright © 2012, Miniwatts Marketing Group

Vocabulary notebook *High-tech gadgets*

Learning tip *Adjective + noun collocations*

When you learn a new compound adjective, find out what nouns you can use after it. Then use the expression to say something true about your life.

not-too-distant future; self-cleaning windows, oven
I hope to graduate in the not-too-distant future.
I'd love a self-cleaning oven and self-cleaning windows.

Dictionary tip

When you look up a compound word in an online dictionary, look at the other items in the drop-down menu as you type. You can often find other useful compounds.

high-p
high-pitched
high-powered

A **Complete each comment with one adjective from the box. Then make the sentences true for you.**

air-conditioned custom-built high-speed labor-saving last-minute

1. We've had high-speed __________ Internet connections in this country for years. High-speed __________ trains, too.
2. I don't live in __________ comfort. It gets hot in the summer, so I'd love an __________ bedroom.
3. I'm always making __________ decisions. I'm always making __________ changes to plans, too.
4. We don't have too many __________ appliances or gadgets, apart from a washing machine.
5. I'd rather have a __________ kitchen than a __________ robot in the house.

B **Find each adjective in Box A in the article on page 22 and write the noun it describes. Then find at least two other nouns in Box B that you can use it with.**

A				B	
energy-efficient	______	______	______	airline	face
carbon-neutral	______	______	______	appliances	food
climate-controlled	______	______	______	car	house
home-cooked	______	______	______	dinner	mall
human-like	______	______	______	environment	sculptures
solar-powered	______	______	______	equipment	travel

C **Word builder** **Complete the compound adjectives in each group with the same word.**

1. wind-______; battery-______; high-______
2. energy-______; cost-______; fuel-______
3. ______-tech; ______- level; ______-class
4. ____-sufficient; ____-explanatory; ____-conscious

D **Focus on vocabulary** **Complete the chart of these words from Exercise 2A on page 27.**

Verb	Noun	Adjective
	adoption	
		cautious
	assumption	
innovate		
	phenomenon	
	revision	

Self, self, self!

The top adjectives with *self* include: *self-sufficient, self-serving, self-conscious, self-explanatory, self-employed, self-taught, self-centered, self-reliant, self-evident*

Unit 3

Society

In Unit 3, you . . .

- talk about different social pressures.
- use participle clauses to link ideas.
- add emphasis with *only, even, so . . . that,* and *such . . . that.*
- change your view as you speak.
- use *even so* and *even then* to introduce contrasting ideas.

Lesson A *Social pressures*

1 Grammar in context

A **What kinds of pressure do people have in their lives? Make a list.**

B CD 1.23 **Listen. What pressures does each person talk about? Are any on your list?**

WE ASKED PEOPLE,

"What are some of the social pressures you've resisted?"

1. CHELSEA, 30 Toronto, Canada, designer

Growing up, I was always branded a rebel, which is a little unfair. I guess, though, that I've never really conformed to social norms, being single and not having had any children at the ripe old age of 30! I just never met anyone, working as hard as I do. But having built up a successful career, I'm happy with my life choices. People say, "Oh, you'll regret it when you're old and lonely." But looking around, I see plenty of elderly people with families who are still lonely.

2. VICTOR, 36 Cancún, Mexico, ex-PR consultant and restaurant owner

I recently decided to get out of the rat race, having been in it most of my adult life. I'd been thinking about doing something different, but then I got laid off and was offered a generous severance package. So, presented with a golden opportunity to change my life, I bought a small restaurant here. Working in the PR industry, people are under enormous pressure, you know, to look good, have the right clothes, and be "perfect," which is really stressful. Not to mention the work hours. I got out. I'm earning less now, running this place, but I just know I'll be a lot happier going forward.

3. CHIN-SUN, 23 Seoul, South Korea, businesswoman

Thinking about it, this is probably going to sound silly, but I feel tremendous pressure to have an active social life. I don't have that many friends compared to my co-workers, or so it seems. I dread Fridays, when they ask if I'm going out with friends on the weekend. And speaking of friends, with social networking, you're supposed to have hundreds of them, and I don't. I mean, not wanting to be rude or anything, I can't see how you can have that many friends, really.

About you

C Pair work **Which of the pressures above are common in your society?**

"I don't think there's a lot of pressure to have kids, but I do think people feel pressure to . . ."

2 Grammar Linking events

Figure it out

A How do the people in the article on page 30 express the ideas below? Rewrite the clauses in bold. Then read the grammar chart.

1. **When I look around**, I see plenty of elderly people with families who are still lonely.
2. I've never really conformed to social norms **because I'm single and haven't had any children.**

Participle clauses

Grammar extra
See page 148.

You can use participle clauses to link events and add information about time or reason.
The subject of the participle clause and the main clause is usually the same.

Present participle	***Growing up,*** *I was always branded a rebel.* (= When I was growing up) *I never met anyone,* ***working as hard as I do.*** (= because I work hard)
Perfect participle	***Having built up a successful career,*** *I'm happy with my life choices.* *I've never conformed to social norms,* ***not having had any children.***

In conversation . . .

Expressions like *generally speaking, thinking about it, bearing in mind, speaking of,* and *talking of* are participle clauses, but they often have a different subject from the main clause.

Bearing in mind the economy, it's no wonder people feel pressured.

B Complete the things the people say about pressures in life. Write participle clauses, using the verbs given. Sometimes there is more than one answer.

1. ________ (be) a woman, I feel a certain pressure to dress well. I mean, ________ (not want) to sound sexist, but unlike my male colleagues, I feel I have to wear something different every day to the office. I think most women do, generally ________ (speak).

2. ________ (grow up) in a family where money was tight, I felt a lot of pressure – especially as a teenager. I used to feel really bad, ________ (not be) able to afford brand-name sneakers or the latest cell phone. So now, ________ (experience) that, and you know, ________ (bear) in mind that kids just want to fit in, I always try to buy my boys the things their friends have.

3. Well, ________ (come) from an academic family, I was to supposed go to a top school. But when I was 18, ________ (work) hard to get the grades I needed, I decided I really wanted to pursue a career as an artist. So, ________ (make up) my mind to do that, I kind of dropped out of formal education altogether. ________ (look back), it was the best decision I ever made.

4. ________ (stay) home and ________ (raise) a family, I've sometimes felt pressure from my friends who work outside the home. They probably think that, ________ (not have) a proper career, I haven't really "done" anything, which is really unfair. I mean, ________ (think) about it, I'd say raising kids is the most important job there is.

About you

C Pair work **Write your view about each comment in Exercise 2B. Then discuss your comments with a partner. What other social pressures are there? Where do these pressures come from?**

"Being a student, I don't really feel any pressure about how to dress. Not having had any fashion sense my entire life, I tend not to worry about these things."

Lesson B *New experiences*

1 Vocabulary in context

A CD 1.24 **What challenges might students face before starting college? Make a list. Then read the web page. How many of your ideas are mentioned?**

So you've graduated from high school and you're ready to take the next step in your academic career. You'll probably be so excited that you can only think of the fun ahead. However, going to college can be such an overwhelming experience that some 35 percent of freshmen drop out in the first year and many leave before the end of the first semester. But don't worry! There are **steps** you can **take** to help you face the challenges and make your first semester both successful and enjoyable.

If, in the first few weeks, you feel so anxious that you only want to **take refuge** in your room, don't. That will only make things even worse. It's only natural to feel like this, and you won't be the only one, so talk to someone about it.

"It takes time to adjust to college life. It may even take most of the first year." –RORY

On the social side, **take advantage of** what college life has to offer. For example, **take part in** extra-curricular activities; take up a new sport or hobby – it's such a great way to meet people that it's worth the effort. However, don't let your social life **take precedence over** your studies. You are there to get a degree, after all.

"Remember to take care of yourself by getting enough sleep. The consequences of sleeping only four hours a night are so huge that you don't even realize till it's too late." –CAITLIN

Academically, it's up to you to **take responsibility for** your studies, and you should **take into account** the fact that you may struggle with new academic challenges. **Take the initiative** and talk to a professor about any problems you have.

"If you don't understand something, ask. **Take charge.**" –ERKAN

In class, learn how to take criticism without taking offense or taking it personally. If you're shy, **take note of** how successful students interact, and use their strategies for participating. If you get a bad grade, **take heart**: it's only one bad grade and is unlikely to throw your studies off course. Even the best students don't always get straight A's.

After the first few weeks, time will go by so fast that your first semester will be over before you know it. Look back and **take stock of** all you've achieved. Then **take credit for** surviving your first semester of college. Good job!

Word sort

B **Find expressions in bold with these meanings, and write them below. Then find other expressions with *take* on the web page. What do they mean? Compare with a partner.**

hide (in) take refuge (in)	take priority (over) ______
have courage or confidence ______	reflect and assess ______
participate, be involved (in) ______	notice ______
take control (of) (2 expressions) ______	accept praise for ______
______	make use of ______
do something positive ______	do something before others do it ______
think about, consider ______	______

About you

C Pair work **Do you agree with the advice given on the web page? What other advice could you give to someone starting college?**

Vocabulary notebook

See page 39.

2 **Grammar** Adding emphasis

Figure it out

A Add one word to each sentence and cross out the underlined words to keep the same meaning. Use the web page to help you. Then read the grammar chart.

1. You may get anxious, and the result will be that you'll take refuge in your room.
2. Taking up a new sport is a good way to make friends, and the result will be that you won't regret it.
3. Adjusting to college may take a year, which is surprising.
4. Before you go to college, you may think about the fun ahead and nothing else.

so . . . that, such (a / an) . . . (that), even, and *only*

Grammar extra *See page 149.*

You can use *so* . . . or *such* . . . (*that*) to emphasize the results or effects of something.
Use *so* . . . + adjective / adverb (*that*) . . . or *such* . . . (*a* / *an*) + (adjective) noun (*that*) . . .
*You'll be **so excited that** you can only think of the fun ahead. Time goes **so fast** you won't notice.*
*It's **such an** overwhelming **experience that** many students drop out.*

Even can add emphasis or signal that something is surprising. *Only* means "no one else" or "nothing else." Use them before the phrase or part of the sentence you want to emphasize.

*You don't **even** realize.* (NOT . . . ~~even don't~~ . . .)	*You **only** want to take refuge in your room.*
*It may **even** take a year to adjust to college life.*	*It will **only** make things worse.*
*That will make things **even** worse.*	*It's **only** natural to feel anxious.*
***Even** the best students don't always get A's.*	***Only** you can take charge of your situation.*

About you

B Complete the conversations with *so . . . that, such (a / an) . . . that, only,* or *even*. If none fit, write a dash (–). Then practice with a partner. Do you agree with the answers? Share your ideas.

1. **What problems do people face when they move to a new city?**

A My friend said he __–__ didn't ______ anticipate how difficult it would be until he moved last year. He said finding an apartment was ______ hard work ______ he ended up taking refuge on a friend's couch. He ______ got a place a month ago. I'd have been ______ depressed ______ I would've given up! It took him ______ long to settle ______ he almost moved back. But he has ______ positive outlook ______ things always work out for him.

B There are probably things you ______ don't ______ take into account – like changing your address on your driver's license. You're usually ______ busy when you move ______ you ______ don't ______ have time to stop and think.

2. **What's it like starting a new job?**

A You know, my first day at this job was ______ big deal ______ I couldn't eat. I ______ felt nervous the week before I started. But you can ______ do your best to fit in. I worked ______ hard my first week ______ it was over before I knew it.

B Well, I'm pretty outgoing, but ______ I get nervous in new job situations. But it ______ lasts a few days. I'd say you should take the initiative to get to know people. Then you'll get ______ involved ______ you'll forget you were ______ nervous. In the end, ______ you can take responsibility for how things turn out.

3 **Viewpoint** Take the initiative

Pair work **Discuss four challenges that people may face in new situations. What advice would you give? Prepare one idea to put on a self-help website.**

"Starting a new job is so stressful for people that they quickly burn out."

Lesson C *Having said that . . .*

1 Conversation strategy Changing views

A **What kinds of peer pressure do young people experience? Make a list.**

B CD 1.25 **Listen. What do Carol and Ashley say are the main pressures on young people today?**

Carol I do think life was a lot easier when I was your age – for young people, I mean.

Ashley You do? In what way?

Carol Well, there wasn't all this peer pressure to have the latest fashions and cell phones and that sort of thing. But having said that, there were other pressures.

Ashley Like what?

Carol Oh, back in the day, women were expected to stay home and raise a family. I mean, some women worked, but even so, their options were limited.

Ashley Well, I guess that's changed, which is good. But then again, they say women still do more of the household chores.

Carol True.

Ashley I think the worst thing now is like pressure to get good grades. You can study and study, but even then, you're not guaranteed a good job at the end of it.

Carol Yes, there's so much competition for jobs nowadays. But then, I suppose there always was.

C **Notice** how Carol and Ashley change their view and express a contrasting view with expressions like these. Find examples in the conversation.

Having said that, (though), . . .
But then, . . .
(But) then again, . . .

D **Link each comment (1–6) with a contrasting view (a–f). Use an expression from Exercise C.**

1. There are so many social problems today.
2. You're not cool if you don't have a car.
3. Getting a good job is a real problem.
4. Looks are important, as is keeping up with the latest trends.
5. And you have to have the latest gadgets.
6. There's so much pressure to do well in school.

a. ______________________, it's hard to live without a cell phone.
b. ______________________, fashion's always been a big thing for a lot of people.
c. ______________________, education was the only way for my parents' generation to get ahead, too.
d. ______________________, you had to have a motorbike to be cool at one time.
e. Having said that, though, there have always been issues to fix in society.
f. ______________________, I don't know anyone who's unemployed.

About you **E** **Pair work** **Take turns starting conversations using the full comments above. Continue each conversation with your own views.**

2 Strategy plus *even so, even then*

CD 1.26 You can use ***even so*** to introduce a contrasting idea. It means, "despite what was just said."

A similar expression is ***even then***, which means "despite the situation that was just described."

A CD 1.27 **Read the comments below. Then listen to people talking about various issues. Predict which comment each person makes next. Number the comments 1–4. There is one extra.**

_______ But even so, they all still want to fit in with their friends.
_______ Even then, I'm sure he got lower grades than he could have – deliberately.
_______ And even then, they're not guaranteed to get a place in college.
_______ Even so, the major problem is that too many kids skip school.
_______ But even so, we still see some cases of this kind of behavior.

About you

B CD 1.28 Pair work **Listen and check your answers. Then discuss the issues with a partner. Do you see these types of problems and peer pressures in your society?**

3 Listening and strategies It's an issue . . .

A CD 1.29 **Discuss the sentences below. Do you agree? Then listen to a conversation. Which sentence best summarizes the main topic of the discussion? Check (✓) the box.**

☐ 1. Parents are just not aware of the issues young people face.
☐ 2. Parents face challenges as their children grow up and become more independent.
☐ 3. Parents and children never used to have conflicts about how children should behave.

B CD 1.30 **Listen again. Complete the contrasting views the speakers give next.**

1. Troy: You shouldn't let kids drive till they're 21.
   Even then, you can't be sure they'll be safe.
2. Troy: Yeah. They're legally old enough at 16 or 17.
   ____
3. Lucy: You even hear of kids texting at the wheel.
   ____
4. Troy: A lot of my friends have stories about their kids growing up too fast. ______________________________
5. Lucy: I think I was an easy kid to raise.
   ____

About you

C Pair work **Discuss the opinions in Exercise B. Do you agree? How else do kids pressure parents? What would you do to resist pressure if you were a parent?**

"Actually, I agree that young people should wait before learning to drive. Though having said that, I guess some kids need to drive at 16, like if they've started working. Even so, it might be better . . ."

Speaking naturally
See page 139

Lesson D *Language and society*

1 Reading

A Prepare **When you study a language, what kinds of things do you learn? Make a list.**

B Read for main ideas **Read the course outlines. Write the title of each course in the space provided. There are two extra titles.**

Language and Social Roles	Accent and Dialect	Right or wrong? Can technology help?
Language and Education	Language Change	What is bilingualism?

Spring semester courses in LANGUAGE and SOCIETY

HOME | PEOPLE | RESEARCH | STUDY | COURSES | RESOURCES

Participants should gain an understanding of how language reflects social structure and social change.

Course 101: ______________________

1 Language is constantly in development, and this course looks at one aspect of this: neologisms, i.e., new words. New words enter the language, sometimes pushing old words out of use. New words are very seldom completely new and are typically made up of existing words or segments of them. Scientific terms such as *nanotechnology* and *psychotherapy* combine classical Latin and Greek roots in new ways. Computer and Internet terminology reuses familiar everyday words, giving them novel meanings (*mouse, friend, memory stick, paste*), and new words are formed from the initial letters of existing words (*RAM, USB*). Sometimes names such as trade names form new words (*to Google*), or words change word class (*a big ask, a must-have*). On other occasions, English simply borrows from other languages (*pizza, sushi*). Such developments reveal a great deal about changes in society.

Course 102: ______________________

2 The purpose of this course is to examine styles of speaking and their social and professional consequences. Everyone speaks with an accent. When we say someone "has no accent," we usually mean the person is using the one associated with people of high social status or education. The term *non-standard accent* refers to geographical / regional varieties of speech, none of which is either inherently superior or inferior to any other. Even so, research shows that people do evaluate regional accents as being more, or less, friendly and pleasant, even judging whether people are suitable for certain types of jobs on the basis of their accent. Additionally, geographical regions and social groups frequently possess their own distinct grammar and vocabulary. However, accents and dialects are increasingly coming under pressure from mass media and centralization, threatening their very existence.

Course 103: ______________________

3 Correct grammar is usually seen as the grammar employed by educated people of higher social status, such as great writers, or those in power. In this course, we use a corpus (a large computer database of recorded conversations and written texts) and dedicated software to investigate thousands of examples of people from every social and educational background speaking and writing. We find there is consensus in that people generally follow the same rules of grammar. Nevertheless, we can also observe numerous cases where everyone seems to "break the rules" without comment. When everyone ignores a grammatical convention, is the rule still valid – or should we rethink it?

Course 104: ______________________

4 Many languages utilize different forms, titles, and names to address people who are friends and intimates, as compared to strangers, superiors, or people with whom a more formal relationship is appropriate. In this course, we examine how English creates, reflects, and maintains social relations. We ask: What is politeness? What is the status of titles and forms of address such as *Professor, Sir, Ma'am*? How do changes in English mirror shifts in social perceptions and relationships? For instance, using gender-marked vocabulary such as *fireman, waitress, chairman* is now regarded as outdated and even offensive by many, and neutral alternatives such as *firefighter, server*, and *chair(person)* are considered more acceptable. What kinds of social structures, therefore, does contemporary English reflect?

About you

C **Read for detail** **Which course covers these questions? Write the course number. Then discuss the questions with a partner.**

1. Does television affect the way people adapt or change the language they use? ________
2. How can examples of actual language be studied? ________
3. Is it possible to avoid sexist language? ________
4. Does the way you speak affect your career prospects? ________
5. What words from foreign languages have been introduced? ________
6. Do native speakers make mistakes? Is this acceptable? ________

2 Focus on vocabulary Synonyms

About you

Find synonyms in the course outlines to replace the words in bold. Then discuss the questions with a partner about your language. Give examples, if possible.

frequently

1. Are new words **often** invented in your language? What are some examples? (101)
2. Which words are **rarely** used anymore? (102)
3. What do you think your **way of speaking** can **show** about you? (102 / 101)
4. Are some accents **seen** as **essentially** good, even **better than** others? (104 / 102 / 102)
5. Are some accents seen as **less good**? (102)
6. Which accents, if any, do people **assess** as being more "friendly"? (102)
   Is there general **agreement** on that? (103)
7. Are there **rules** for addressing people of different social status, gender, or age? (103)
8. Do people of higher social status use language that is **different**? (102)

3 Listening and speaking Language and gender

A CD 1.31 **Read the outline below. Can you predict the missing words? Then listen and complete each sentence with one, two, or three words.**

Course 105 Language and Gender

A controversial and ________________ area, this course analyzes language and gender on the basis of facts or ________________. Questions include: Do men ________________ more than women? Are women less assertive or less ________________? Researching such questions, we find ________________ difference between the sexes, so should we instead consider who is dominant? Put simply, people of a ________________ talk more. We also look at "sexist" language and whether communication between the sexes is ________________. Finally, we ask: Do comparisons imply that one type of talk is ________________ another?

B CD 1.32 **Listen again and answer the questions. Write notes.**

1. Why does the professor advise the students to read only the books on the reading list?
2. In Lecture 1, what question will be considered in addition to the ones in the outline?
3. Lecture 2 will cover studies that found that men talk more. Why is that?
4. In Lecture 3, what is one of the examples given of possibly "sexist" language?
5. Lecture 4 is about Tannen's work. Why does she say men and women's language is different?
6. In Lecture 5, what does the professor say should be studied instead of male–female differences?

About you

C **Pair work** **Discuss which lecture you think sounds most interesting. What views do you have on men and women's language? Are there issues of sexist language in your language?**

"Actually the Language and Gender course sounds really interesting. Not having studied it before, I think I'd learn a lot about how men and women communicate."

Writing *I recommend it.*

In this lesson, you . . .
- plan and write an evaluative report.
- express results in writing.
- avoid errors with *therefore*.

Task **Write a report on a course.**

Write an evaluation of an international summer course you attended, taking into account other students' positive and negative views. Make a recommendation for future students.

A Look at a model **Look at some students' comments on a course. Check (✓) the comments that are included in the report. Would you put the other points in paragraph 2 or 3? Write the number.**

STUDENTS' COMMENTS

- ☐ Good food, accommodations
- ☐ We enjoyed the group work
- ☐ Some lectures were too long
- ☐ One professor talked too fast
- ☐ Too much reading
- ☐ Campus too far from city
- ☐ Good social program and good to meet other students
- ☐ Difficult assignments

The purpose of this report is to evaluate the residential Business Management Program, which I attended in July. As requested, I will report on both the positive and negative aspects.

On the positive side, the course was extremely well designed, giving all students an opportunity to take part. Group work was an integral part of the program. As a result, the classes were lively and varied. In terms of the social program, everyone enjoyed meeting people from other countries, making many new friends in the process.

On the negative side, some students complained that there was too much reading, leaving little time for evening activities. A further complaint was that one professor spoke so quickly that some students could not understand her.

In conclusion, the course was both useful and enjoyable. Having said that, there are some aspects which should be changed, such as the amount of reading. Even so, it was an excellent course, and I would therefore recommend it to other students.

B Focus on language **Read the chart. Then underline the examples of results in Exercise A.**

Expressing results in writing

You can express a result in writing with present participle clauses, *so / such . . . that . . .*, or *so*.
There was too much reading, ***leaving little time for evening activities.***
She spoke ***so*** *quickly* ***that*** *students could not understand her.* OR *She spoke quickly,* ***so*** *students . . .*

You can also use *as a result, consequently,* or *therefore*.
Group work was part of the course. ***As a result, / Consequently,*** *the classes were lively.*
It was an excellent course, and I would ***therefore*** *recommend it.*

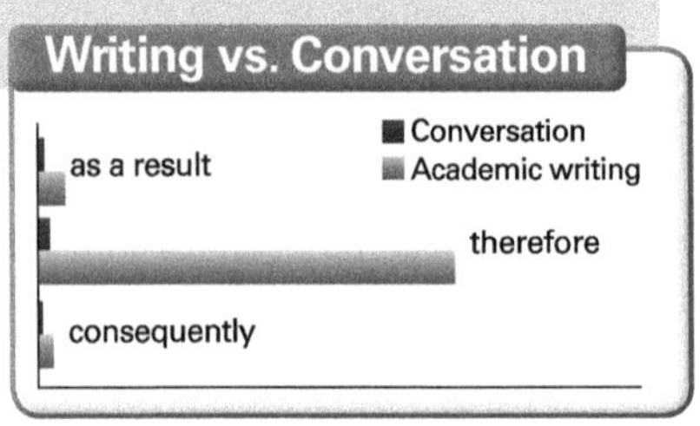

C **Rewrite the sentences, using the structures given.**

1. The teacher spoke too fast. This made it difficult for students to follow. (participle)
2. The campus was too far from the city. We were only able to go there once. (*so . . . that* or *so*)
3. Some lectures were too long. This left no time for questions. (participle)
4. There was a good mix of nationalities. English was widely used. (*Consequently* or *As a result*)
5. The accommodations were excellent. We recommend staying on campus. (*therefore*)

D Write and check **Write an evaluation of a course that you have taken. Use Exercises A and C to help you. Then check for errors.**

Common errors

Do not use *therefore* by itself to join two clauses.
It was excellent. ***Therefore****, I would recommend it.* OR
It was excellent, ***and therefore,*** *I would recommend it.*
(NOT ~~*It was excellent therefore I would recommend it.*~~)

Vocabulary notebook *Take credit!*

Learning tip **Paraphrase**

When you learn an expression, write it in a sentence that paraphrases the meaning. It will help you remember the meaning of the expression.

take the initiative

I need to take the initiative on a project at work, and start it without waiting for my co-workers.

A **Complete the sentences with the correct expressions from the box. Use the underlined paraphrases to help you.**

take advantage of	take credit for	take into account	take part in	take responsibility for

1. It's good to ________________ events that your friends organize and join in what they are doing.
2. I should ________________ being single and make the most of the fact that I have few responsibilities.
3. When you see some teens behaving badly, you should ________________ how easily they can be influenced and consider the peer pressure they are under.
4. If I do something wrong, I have to ________________ it and take the blame for it.
5. You should ________________ the good things you do in your community because it's important to know how to accept praise and be recognized.

B **Use each expression in a sentence and paraphrase its meaning.**

1. take heart ________________
2. take precedence ________________
3. take refuge in ________________
4. take steps ________________
5. take stock of ________________
6. take note of ________________

C **Word builder** **Find the meanings of these expressions. Write each one in a sentence, and write a paraphrase of its meaning.**

take action	take place	take for granted
take exception to	take effect	take issue (with)
take into consideration		

What we take!

The top collocations of *take* include:
take care, advantage, place, seriously, step(s), precedence, for granted, account, action.

D **Focus on vocabulary** **Look at the course outlines on page 36. Find words for the paraphrases in bold. Then write sentences using the words and giving examples. Refer to Exercise 2 on page 37 to help you.**

Give an example of . . .

1. something you **don't often** do and something you **often** do.
2. an issue on which there is **agreement** in your group of friends.
3. something you **think of** as very important in life.
4. something you do that **shows or makes evident** your personality.
5. a **way that something is usually done** in society that you don't agree with.
6. how people **judge** you by your **way of speaking** or how you dress.
7. an area in your country that has very **different** pronunciation.
8. something that you feel is **essentially** dangerous.
9. a thing you own that is **better than** a friend's and something that is **not as good**.

Checkpoint 1 *Units 1–3*

1 Peer pressure

A Circle the correct auxiliary verb. Then complete the sentences with an appropriate adverb from the box. Sometimes there is more than one answer.

evidently	inevitably	ironically	presumably
ideally	invariably	potentially	supposedly

1. *A* My friend says she feels a lot of pressure from her parents, as I **am / do**, really. You know, to take all these extra classes, play an instrument, do a sport. I mean, do you?
   B Oh, yeah. ________, our parents never did all this stuff. ________, they just want us to have more opportunities than they **did / are**. Well, I know my mom **is / does**.
2. *A* There's ________ all this bullying in schools. But you know, I've never experienced it. And I know my friends **haven't / have**, either. Have you?
   B Well, ________, a lot of it happens online. So ________, you don't see a lot of it. And our school has a strict policy on bullying, which a lot of schools **does / do**, I suppose.
3. *A* I don't really feel any strong peer pressure, though my best friend **does / is**. Do you?
   B Well, there's ________ some. My friends are all pretty confident, but I **do / am**, too.
   A That's good. I mean, ________, you want supportive friends. Well, I **have / do**. Some people are always worrying about what others think – as my friend **is / are**. And ________, that's bad for you.

About you

B Pair work **Ask and answer the questions in Exercise A. Use *even so* and *even then*.**

"Actually, my parents don't pressure me at all. But even so, I still want to do well so I don't disappoint them. So yeah, I try to get good grades and everything."

2 Using technology

A Complete the comments using *to, not to, one,* or *ones*. Complete the underlined idioms.

1. There's software on my computer that I don't know how to use. And I'll probably never be able ________. I mean, I'd like ________, but . . . it's ________ me.
2. You know, my phone has all these useless functions. Like the most useless ________ for most people is the stock market report. I don't see ________ it.
3. I can't use the remote to record anything. Well, I could, but I prefer ________. I can't make heads ________ it. And I always mess up the satellite channels when I try ________.
4. We want to get one of those things that cleans your floors. Well, we were going ________. Oh, what are they called? It's on the tip ________ – those, um, robot things.
5. We never had calculators in my day. Not like the ________ they have now. You had to learn all your math tables by ________. You just had to come ________ with it all.
6. A gadget I can't live without? I don't know off the top ________. Nothing comes ________. I'd like to get a scooter, but I'll never be able ________. The ________ I want is so expensive.

About you

B Pair work **Discuss the comments above. Are any true for you? Express a contrasting view with expressions like *Having said that, But then,* and *(But) then again*.**

"I have no idea how to use spreadsheets, but I'd like to. Having said that, I'm not sure I need to."

3 Bookworms

A Complete the *take* expressions in both interviews. Then in 1, write participle clauses using the verbs given. In 2, write *both . . . and, either . . . or, neither . . . nor,* or *not only . . . but also.*

1. ________ (grow up), I was always a bookworm. Reading always **took** ________ **over** everything else. If I **take** ________ **of** all my successes in life, it's probably due to reading. My mom has to **take** ________ **for** teaching us to read. ________ (not have) a career, she stayed home and **took** ________ **for** our education. She used to **take** ________ **of** how much we read every day. And ________ (live) near a library, we always **took** ________ **of** it. By the age of 10, I had a wide vocabulary, ________ (read) as much as I did. I often won the local spelling bees when I **took** ________ **in** them. Also, ________ (read) all the classics, I was good at general-knowledge quizzes, too. These days, ________ (work) as much as I do, I still like to **take** ________ **in** a book. It's a great way to escape from life!
2. I haven't read ________ a book ________ a magazine in months. Well, unless you **take into** ________ the books I read to my kids. They want me ________ to read every night ________ to tell them stories about when I was a kid. So I read and tell stories every single night. Sometimes I have ________ the time ________ the energy after a day's work. But even if you are busy, you can **take** ________ to help your kids read. Like now they have electronic readers for kids, which are great. They're ________ fun ________ educational. Kids can ________ read ________ listen at the same time. If they don't know how to say a word, they can ________ ask me ________ point to it and hear it. It's a great way to get kids to **take the** ________ and read.

About you

B Pair work **Discuss the ideas above. Use expressions like *I do think* to add emphasis.**

"I do think it's good for parents to read to their kids."

4 Solar power

A How many compound adjectives do you remember? Make a list. Then use them to discuss different technologies with a partner. Use *can't possibly* and *couldn't possibly.*

"I bet a lot of people couldn't possibly live without their labor-saving devices."

B Circle the correct options to complete the information from a website selling solar-power panels.

Worried about heating costs? **If so, / If not**, why not install solar panels in your home to reduce your energy bills? They are now **such / so** affordable that everyone can benefit from them. And what's just as important, **if not / if so** more important, is that it's **such / so** a clean source of power that you'll be helping to reduce pollution, too. With some systems, you can **even / so** get paid for the energy you produce. The panels **such / only** take a day to install. Your heating bills will fall **so / such** rapidly that you'll be pleased that you've made **so / such** a great investment.

C Rewrite the comments using the phrases in parentheses.

1. I know there are a lot of people for solar energy. (happy to pay)
2. Solar power is not a cheap technology, or so I heard. (to install)
3. The people have it, and they said it cost a fortune. (next door)
4. Solar panels change the look of your home. (on the roof)
5. It's definitely something because it saves money. (to be considered)
6. People will be disappointed. (hoping to get their money back quickly)
7. I also heard that some homes can't have it. (built before a certain date)

Unit 4

Amazing world

In Unit 4, you . . .

- talk about the natural world.
- use the future perfect and future perfect continuous.
- use prepositional expressions like *due to* and *far from*.
- add ideas with expressions like *what's more* and *not to mention*.
- use *in any case* to state conclusions or add information.

Lesson A *Animal behavior*

1 Vocabulary in context

A **Which creatures (animals, birds, insects) do you find interesting? Lovable? Scary?**

B CD 2.02 **Listen and read the excerpts from a nature documentary. Complete the photo captions with these words: a. breeding, b. hibernation, c. migration.**

Animal Behavior

Every September, the arctic tern leaves its **breeding grounds** in the Arctic and heads south to the Antarctic. When it arrives back in the Northern Hemisphere the next summer, it will have flown on average 70,000 kilometers (almost 44,000 miles), which means by the end of its thirty-year lifespan, the arctic tern will have flown the equivalent of three round trips to the moon.

The longest ______________

In order to **survive the winter months**, many small mammals **store food** before they **go into hibernation**. Groundhogs, however, **build up** their fat **reserves** and then **dig a burrow**, where they **hibernate** until spring. By the time the groundhog is in its deep sleep, its heartbeat will have dropped from 80 to 4 beats per minute and its body temperature will have fallen to only a few degrees above the outside temperature. By the time spring arrives, if it has not been **attacked** by **predators**, the groundhog will have been hibernating for almost six months.

Groundhog
____

After **mating**, a female emperor penguin **lays** a single **egg** before returning to the ocean, where she **feeds** and spends the winter. Penguins don't **build nests**. Instead, the male emperor balances the **egg** on his feet, huddling together with other males in the **colony** to **keep warm**. By the time the females return, these male penguins will have been protecting the eggs for 65 days. They won't have eaten for 115 days and will have lost nearly half of their body weight. Once the **eggs hatch**, the females **feed** and **raise the young**, while the males head to the ocean to feed.

The ______________ habits of emperor penguins

Word sort

C **Copy the chart and write the bold words and collocations in the documentary. Add others you want to learn. Which facts did you know? Which didn't you know? Tell a partner.**

survival (food and sleep)	having young	homes and groups
feed	lay an egg	

"I knew that penguins lay eggs, but I didn't know that they only lay single eggs."

Vocabulary notebook

See page 51.

2 **Grammar** Talking about the past in the future

A Circle the correct verb form in the sentences. Use the documentary to help you. Then read the grammar chart.

1. By the time a penguin egg hatches, the emperor male **will have lost / will lose** half his body weight.
2. By the time spring arrives, the groundhog **will be hibernating / will have been hibernating** for six months.

Future perfect and future perfect continuous

Grammar extra
See page 150.

You can use future perfect forms for events that are in the past when you view them from the future.

Use the simple form to suggest that an event will be complete before a certain time.	*How far **will** the tern **have flown**?* *It **will have flown** 70,000 kilometers by the time it arrives back in the Arctic.*
Use the continuous form to suggest that an event will be in progress at a particular time in the future.	*How long **will** it **have been hibernating**?* *By then, it **will have been hibernating** for six months.*

Common errors

Do not use the future perfect in *if* or time clauses.
*When it **arrives** back, it will have flown 70,000 kilometers. If it **has not been attacked** . . .*
(NOT ~~*When it will have arrived back*~~ . . .)
(NOT ~~*If it will not have been attacked*~~ . . .)

B Complete these excerpts from the documentary. Use a future perfect form of the verbs given. Sometimes there is more than one correct answer.

1. It's winter in Canada and too cold for the monarch butterfly to feed and survive. So it starts its journey south, and by the time it arrives in Mexico, it __will have flown__ (fly) more than 4,000 kilometers (2,485 miles).
2. Giant pandas almost exclusively eat bamboo. At the end of the day, when it finishes feeding, it ________________ (eat) 40 pounds of bamboo and it ________________ (forage) for 16 hours.
3. These gray whales are leaving their feeding grounds in the cooler north to breed in the warmer south. When they reach Mexican waters, they ________________ (swim) 160 kilometers (about 100 miles) a day for 8 to 10 weeks.
4. After mating at sea, female leatherback turtles come ashore. It's here that they dig a hole, and by the end of the night, they ________________ (lay) 80 or more eggs.
5. Some bald eagle nests weigh more than a ton. But by the time they reach this weight, the bald eagles ________________ (add) sticks to the nest for several years.
6. This female elephant is heavily pregnant. By the time she is ready to give birth, she ________________ (carry) the baby for over 22 months.

C Pair work **Take turns asking and answering questions about the facts in Exercise B. How much can you remember?**

3 **Viewpoint** A wildlife presentation

Pair work **Choose a creature that interests you, and prepare a presentation. Take turns giving your presentations to the class. What new facts do you learn?**

"By the time this penguin reaches the open sea, it will have traveled more than 50 miles across the frozen ice."

Lesson B *Desert landscapes*

1 Grammar in context

A What do you know about deserts? Make a class list.

The largest hot desert in the world is the Sahara.

B CD 2.03 **Listen to extracts from a geography lecture about deserts. Which three slides does the professor refer to? Number the slides 1–3. There is one extra slide.**

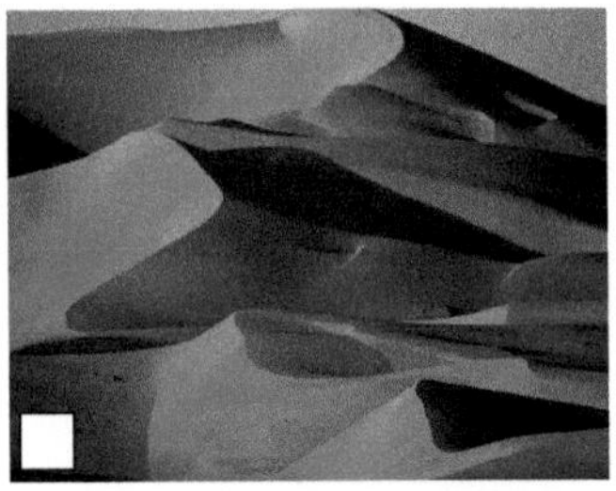

1 "Deserts are, for lack of a better description, among some of the most fascinating and diverse landscapes on earth. They cover approximately one-third of the earth's land surface and stretch across all continents. But what is a desert? Most people think of them as hot, sandy places thanks to photographs of sand dunes in the Sahara desert. But in fact, only about 10 percent of the world's deserts are covered with sand dunes, including the Sahara. In line with USGS* definitions, a desert is an area that has less than 250 millimeters (10 inches) of rain per year. So Antarctica is a desert, apart from being one of the coldest places on earth. And in addition to cold deserts, there are also mountainous deserts.". . .

2 "Deserts are also commonly believed to be wastelands, on account of their harsh living conditions for wildlife and plants. But far from being barren, deserts are often very rich in plant life. Death Valley in the United States has over 1,000 plant species in spite of the fact that it has some of the most extreme conditions. And many species of animals can also survive in a desert climate by virtue of having adapted to the environment. Some, like the camel, can go up to eight days without drinking. As for smaller mammals, many have adapted by means of living underground or by hunting only at night.". . .

3 "One problem with deserts is that they expand and encroach on arable land. In fact, there is great concern in many parts of the world about this process, known as "desertification." Take for example the Gobi desert, which has spread, in part due to the fact that agricultural practices have changed from those in use prior to the 1950s. China was faced with increasing areas of arid land in place of its valuable grasslands. And, as a result of experiencing increasingly severe dust storms, China has started planting trees with the aim of halting desertification. By the end of the planned 70-year project, they will have planted more than 4,500 kilometers (approximately 2,800 miles) of trees."

*United States Geological Survey

C Complete the sentences with information from the lecture. Then replace the underlined words with an expression from the lecture. In some, more than one expression can be used.

1. Most people think of deserts as ________ places because of photographs of the Sahara.
2. According to USGS definitions, a desert is an area that ________.
3. As well as cold deserts, there are also ________ deserts.
4. Deserts are not at all barren and can be ________.
5. Many animals can ________ in a desert climate through their adaptation to the environment.
6. As well as larger animals like ________, there are many small mammals that live in the desert.
7. The Gobi desert has spread because of farming practices that didn't exist before ________.

2 Grammar Combining ideas

Figure it out

A How does the professor express the ideas below in her lecture? Rewrite the sentences.

1. Deserts are believed to be wastelands because they have harsh living conditions.
2. Antarctica is a desert although it is one of the coldest places on earth.
3. Death Valley has over 1,000 plant species even though it has some of the most extreme conditions.

Prepositions

Grammar extra *See page 151.*

Prepositions can be a word or a phrase. They can be followed by a noun phrase or an *-ing* form.
***In line with** USGS definitions, a desert has less than 250 millimeters of rain **per** year.*
*A camel can go up to eight days **without drinking**.*

If a preposition starts an *-ing* clause, the verb has the same subject as the verb in the main clause.
***As a result of** experiencing severe dust storms, China started planting trees.*

Some prepositions can be followed by *the fact that* + a clause. Use *the fact that* if the subject changes.
*Antarctica is a desert, apart from **the fact that it is** one of the coldest places on earth.*
*The Gobi desert has spread due **to the fact** that agricultural practices have changed.*

B Rewrite the sentences. Replace the underlined ideas with the expressions given, and make any other necessary changes. Some have more than one correct answer.

1. It is not true that deserts are unpopulated – they are home to almost one-sixth of the world's population. (Far from) Far from being unpopulated, deserts are home to . . .
2. Many animals burrow underground to avoid the harsh sun, and they are nocturnal. (In addition to)
3. Plants such as cacti not only have long roots, but they can store their own water. (Apart from)
4. Some desert plants survive for hundreds of years because of these kinds of adaptations. (thanks to)
5. Many desert areas are expanding because humans graze animals in semi-arid areas. (on account of)
6. Environmentalists are concerned that these farming practices have caused desertification. (about)

3 Listening The Antarctic

A CD 2.04 **Listen to Part 1 of an exclusive interview with an expert on the Antarctic. Complete the interviewer's notes. What else do you learn about the climate there?**

Temperatures in degrees centigrade	Lowest ever	Summer	Winter	
	Minus ______	______	______	

B CD 2.05 **Guess which sentences are true. Then listen to Part 2 and circle T (True) or F (False).**

1. Antarctica is different from everywhere else on the planet – even the Arctic. **T / F**
2. Antarctica has been cold for over 30 million years. **T / F**
3. Scientists study Antarctica to see if there could be life on other planets. **T / F**
4. Some fish and animals survive in Antarctica thanks to antifreezes in their bloodstream. **T / F**
5. On one of the expert's visits to Antarctica, 18 people shared one tomato. **T / F**

Lesson C What's more . . .

1 Conversation strategy Adding ideas

A Match words from a conversation with definitions. Guess the topic of the conversation.

1. overfishing ____	a. not interested and unconcerned
2. species ____	b. exploiting fish to the extent that they can't replace themselves
3. apathetic ____	c. government money used to help projects that are beneficial to the public
4. subsidies ____	d. a class or group of individuals that are related to one another

B CD 2.06 Listen to a seminar discussion. What factors contributed to the problem of overfishing?

Julio Well, the biggest issue seems to have been overfishing. Something like three-quarters of the world's fish species have been completely exploited. It's only a matter of time before the fishing industry collapses completely.

Maria Not to mention all the other industries that depend on it. So who or what's responsible for it all?

Julio Well, the international community has been increasing fishing capacity, for one thing . . .

Ulma And additionally, governments give subsidies, so large-scale fishing operations took over. And big commercial fleets are much more efficient at finding fish as well.

Maria And on top of that, I guess consumers got used to having a wide variety of fish available, so the demand was there. Also, fish became much more affordable.

Ulma What's more, the public has, to a large extent, been pretty apathetic. And then industry has been slow to respond to concerns. In any case, apathy has contributed to the problem.

C **Notice** how the students use expressions like these to add and focus on a new idea. Find the ones they use.

Also, . . .	*Additionally, . . .*
And then . . .	*In addition, . . .*
. . . as well	*What's more, . . .*
. . . not to mention . . .	*On top of that, . . .*

D CD 2.07 Listen to more of the discussion. Write the missing expressions. Then practice.

Julio True. And of course another problem is all the pollution that runs into the oceans.

Maria Yeah, ____________ the amount of trash that's dumped in them. Apparently, there's a huge trash pile in the middle of the Pacific that you can see from space. ____________, whales and dolphins can eat that stuff.

Ulma And ____________, it's irresponsible, dumping waste where we get our food.

Maria ____________, all that pollution is changing the chemistry of the ocean, which affects the lifecycle of fish. ____________, it has an impact on shellfish. Coral ____________.

Ulma ____________ there's the issue of meltwater from the ice caps caused by rising temperatures.

Julio There's a lot of debate about that, but in any event, it's impacting the ocean.

2 Strategy plus *In any case, in any event*

CD 2.08 You can use ***in any case*** to add more information to make an argument stronger or clearer.

You can also use ***in any case*** or ***in any event*** when you reach a conclusion that you think is the only possible one.

In conversation . . .

In any case is more frequent.

In any case ■■■■
In any event ■

CD 2.09 **Find two appropriate conclusions for each conversation. Write the letters a–f. Then listen and check your answers. Practice with a partner.**

1. *A* It seems like global warming is still a controversial issue. But don't scientists all agree that temperatures are rising? And what's more, that it affects the oceans with sea levels rising?
   B I suppose the controversy is about what's *causing* the increase in temperatures. ______ ______
2. *A* You know what's interesting to me? We really don't know that much about the oceans.
   B Yeah, though they're making new discoveries all the time.
   A Yeah, no. They definitely know more now than, say, 20 years ago. ______ ______
3. *A* There are some amazing creatures in the ocean, like jellyfish that glow in the dark.
   B I know. Not to mention the ones that can kill you, like the box jellyfish.
   A Actually, there are a lot of poisonous creatures in the ocean. Like, well, I can't think. ______ ______

a. In any event, there's definitely evidence that the atmosphere is getting warmer.
b. But in any event, there are lots of species we haven't discovered yet.
c. But in any event, there are a lot of deadly things in there.
d. In any case, you have to be careful in some places when you go swimming.
e. In any case, there's no doubt that the climate is changing.
f. Though we haven't made it to the bottom. In any event, we're a long way from fully exploring it.

3 Strategies The human impact on nature

About you

A Add an idea to each comment below. Include an expression from Exercise 1C.

1. I think humans do a lot to protect nature and wildlife. For example, if we didn't have zoos, we probably wouldn't be able to preserve some species. What's more, . . .
2. Well, one of the ways we impact nature is by building homes on sensitive areas, like wetlands. That forces the wildlife out of their natural habitats.
3. I think in many ways we've forgotten how to live with nature. You know, by the time they graduate from high school, one in three kids won't have been on a hike or seen a forest.

B Pair work **Discuss the ideas in Exercise A. Add more ideas to each conversation, and draw conclusions using *in any case* or *in any event*.**

A I'm not so sure it's good to keep animals in zoos.
B Yeah, but zoos have programs to help endangered species. And on top of that, . . .

Speaking naturally
See page 139.

Lesson D *Biomimicry*

1 Reading

A Prepare **Look at the title of the article and the photos. What do you think *biomimicry* is?**

B Read for main ideas **Read the article. What inventions has nature inspired?**

How NATURE *inspires* SCIENCE —a look at some notable inventions

By the end of this century, as one looks back on the multitude of achievements, one may be surprised to find that a number of technological and scientific advances will be based upon observations in nature, as opposed to accidental discovery or a result of trial and error in a laboratory.

A relatively new field of research, called biomimicry, is providing significant insights and solutions for scientists and inventors in areas from medicine and technology to transportation and construction.

Using nature to solve design problems is not new. The Wright brothers observed the flight of birds while building their plane. However, in recent years, biomimicry has become an established discipline among scientists, and one that is generating some remarkable inventions. Here are some that in the not-too-distant future will have had a considerable impact on our lives.

1. SHARKSKIN A University of Florida engineering professor noticed that sharkskin remains amazingly clean and that plants and sea animals have difficulty adhering to it. He created a pattern that mimics the shark's tiny scales. Apart from the fact that it was up to 85 percent cleaner than smooth surfaces, it also prevented harmful bacteria from sticking to it.

The result was a material that can be used for hospital tray tables and bed rails, as well as other areas where there is a high risk of passing on infections. In several years, it is likely that Professor Brennan's invention will have had demonstrable benefits in terms of reducing hospital-acquired infections, and it will undoubtedly have saved thousands of lives.

2. TERMITE MOUNDS A Zimbabwean architect was faced with the difficult task of finding a workable solution to the problem of designing a new building that would stay cool even without air conditioning. Looking for an affordable alternative, he found his inspiration in African termite mounds. He noticed that the mounds termites build catch air at the base and circulate it up through their mud home. As a result of replicating the system in his building, he reduced energy costs by a measurable amount. His building uses one-tenth of the energy of similar buildings and shows that there is a viable alternative to using air-conditioning systems.

3. GECKO FEET For human beings, walking up walls is the stuff of movies – unimaginable in real life. Or is it? Inspired by the millions of tiny hairs on gecko feet, scientists are working hard to produce a "gecko tape" to use on the soles of footwear. The tape mimics the hairs on the gecko's feet and is a powerful and dependable adhesive. Scientists hope to have a product for space stations and underwater applications in the near future. And who knows? By the end of the century, they may have created a boot that enables us all to climb buildings like Spiderman. Imagine how profitable that would be!

C React Pair work **Look back at the article. Discuss the questions with a partner.**

- What do you think about biomimicry as a science?
- Which of the inventions in the article do you think is most exciting? Most valuable? Why?
- What other applications can you think of for the sharkskin material? How about for the gecko tape?

2 Focus on vocabulary Suffixes with *-able*

A **Read the article again. Circle the words that end in *-able*. Then replace the words in bold with a word from the article ending in *-able* that has a similar meaning.**

1. Studying nature has led human beings to some **amazing** scientific inventions. ____ remarkable
2. A **large** number of inventions initially failed. ____
3. People using biomimicry in the past is **hard to imagine**. ____
4. When it comes to preventing harmful bacteria from sticking to it, the sharkskin material is very **reliable**. ____
5. The sharkskin material has had a **clear** effect on hospital infection rates. (2 words) ____
6. One of the most **noteworthy** inventions is a fabric that mimics a butterfly's shiny wings. ____
7. The architect came up with a **practical** plan for keeping buildings cool. (2 words) ____
8. The gecko tape is not likely to be a **feasible** or **money-making** invention. (2 words) ____
9. Many of the inventions are not **expensive to produce**. ____

B **Do the statements above agree with the information in the article? Write Y (Yes), N (No), or NG (Information not given).**

C Pair work **Share what you learned about biomimicry using the *-able* words in Exercise A.**

3 Listening and speaking The genius of the natural world

A CD 2.10 **Listen to a presentation about the applications of biomimicry. Match the examples from nature that the presenter talks about to the real-world problems below. Number the pictures 1–4.**

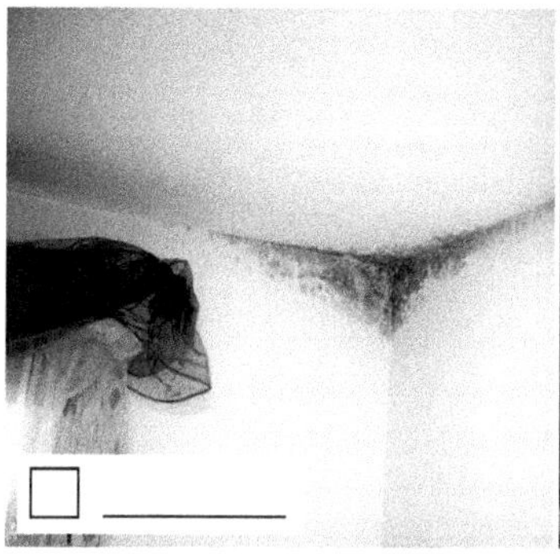

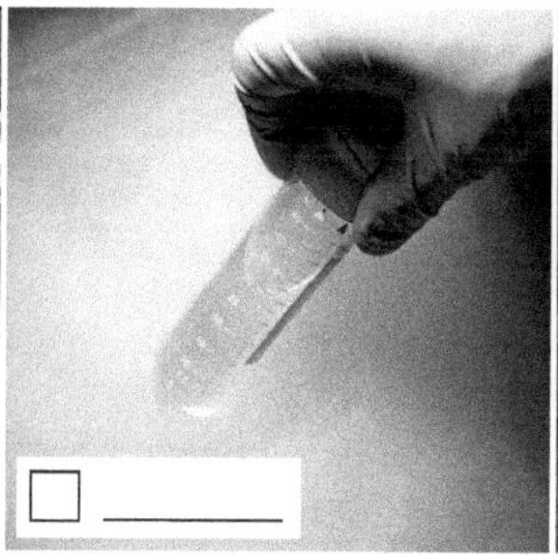

B CD 2.11 **Listen again. Have the problems already been solved? Write Y (Yes) or N (No) on each picture above.**

About you

C Group work **Look back at the examples in the lesson. How else could the ideas be applied to real-world problems? What other amazing things are in nature? What problems could they solve?**

"Maybe in the future scientists will have developed a material that cleans itself, like that flower. If they used it on cars, you would never have to clean your car."

Writing *Does it matter?*

In this lesson, you . . .

- write a persuasive essay.
- use academic prepositions and *one.*
- avoid errors with *upon.*

Task Write an essay.

The World Animal Foundation estimates that by 2025 as many as one-fifth of all animal species may well have become extinct. Does this matter?

A Look at a model **Read the introductions to two essays that answer the question above. What view does each one take? What arguments does each one make?**

1. The estimate that 20 percent of animal species may disappear within a short time is alarming. The loss of any species matters because it can upset the balance of nature. Each organism depends upon another to survive, and the disappearance of one species may have unknown consequences for another. The earth maintains a delicate balance, which relies upon the complex interaction of plant and animal species. We do not always see what is happening beneath the surface. The loss of species may be a warning that we are destroying our planet and therefore our very existence.

2. The claim that a large proportion of animal species is at risk of dying out is a subject of great debate within the academic community and amongst scientists in particular. One might think that this is a major problem and that one's worst fears for the earth will materialize. However, one can equally argue that species have become extinct throughout the history of this planet. In terms of our survival, however, this has not proved critical. Therefore, the extinction of species, far from being a disaster, can simply be considered part of the normal evolutionary process.

Question-based essays

Show you understand the question by restating it in your own words. Give your opinion in your introduction and conclusion.

B Focus on language **Read the chart. Then underline the examples of formal prepositions and circle examples of *one* for general statements in Exercise A.**

Prepositions in academic writing; *one* for general statements

Some prepositions and prepositional expressions can make your writing sound more formal, e.g., *amongst, beneath, throughout, upon, within, in terms of.*
Each organism depends ***upon*** *another.*
It is a subject of debate ***within*** *the academic community and* ***amongst*** *scientists. . . .*
In terms of *our survival, this has not proved critical.*

One / one's can refer to "people in general" or "you / your." You can use it to give opinions.
One *might think this is a major problem and that* ***one's*** *worst fears will materialize.*

C **Complete the sentences with prepositions. Then rewrite them using *one / one's.***

1. A healthy environment is dependent ________ how well people manage their resources.
2. We should do everything ________ our power to protect these species.
3. There are complex systems ________ the earth's surface that people do not fully understand.
4. I wonder how the leopard and rhino, which are ________ the most threatened species, can survive.
5. The effects ________ tourism will be so huge ________ the world that we cannot imagine them.

D Write and check **Write an essay to answer the question in the task above. Then check for errors.**

Common errors

Do not overuse *upon.* Use it after *depend, rely, agree. Look upon* means "to think about in a certain way," not "look at."
Let us look at this subject in more detail. (NOT. . . ~~*look upon*~~ . . .)

Vocabulary notebook *Golden eggs*

Learning tip **Specialized vocabulary**

When you learn vocabulary from a specific area such as animal behavior, find out if it has other uses in general English or in idioms.

hibernate

Animals hibernate or sleep in the winter.

Computers hibernate when they're running but are not being used.

A Complete each sentence with a word in the box. Sometimes you'll use a word twice.

breed	colony	grounds	lays	migration	predator
burrow	feed and raise	~~hatch~~	mate	nest	young

1. When eggs hatch, baby birds, fish, or insects come out.
   If you plan something in secret, you hatch **a plan**.
2. Animals that ________ for life stay together forever.
   A presidential candidate chooses **a running** ________, who becomes vice president if elected.
3. In academic writing, the offspring, or babies, of animals are called their ________.
   You can also use the expression **the** ________ to mean all young people.
4. A ________ is a group of birds or animals.
   It can also be a country that is governed by a more powerful country.
5. A ________ is a place where most birds have their young.
   A ________ **egg** is a sum of money you save for a special purpose.
6. When animals ________, they have young. A specific type of animal is also called a ________.
   If you say someone or something is part of **a dying** ________, it means there aren't many left.
7. Breeding, feeding, fishing, or hunting ________ are places where these activities take place.
   To have ________ for something means to have reasons for it, such as ________ **for divorce**.
8. To ________ means to dig into something and a ________ can be the hole where an animal lives.
   A person can also ________ into something. It means he or she investigates it.
9. The movement of birds, animals, or people is called ________.
   From that word, we get other words like *immigrant*, *emigrate*, etc.
10. A bird, a fish, or an insect ________ an egg.
    Someone that makes a lot of money for others is called **the goose that** ________ **the golden egg**.
11. In biology, a ________ is an animal that attacks and eats other animals.
    In business, it's a company that tries to buy or take over other companies.
12. Both animals and humans have to ________ their families.

B Word builder Here are some more idioms with animals. Find out their meaning.

be a guinea pig	beat a dead horse	clam up	have ants in your pants
be in the doghouse	be a fish out of water	get off your high horse	have butterflies in your stomach

C Focus on vocabulary Can you think of a thing or person for each expression? See Exercise 2A, page 49.

1. a **remarkable** animal that has **considerable** intelligence ________
2. a **dependable** source of information or a **notable** authority on the natural world ________
3. something you've learned about nature that previously was **unimaginable** to you ________
4. a **viable** or workable alternative to fossil fuels ________
5. an **affordable** way to experience nature ________
6. a **profitable** product with **measurable** results that resulted from replicating nature ________

Unit 5

Progress

In Unit 5, you . . .

- talk about inventions, progress, and human achievements.
- use adverbs with continuous and perfect passives.
- use modal verbs with passive forms.
- make a point with expressions like *I look at it this way.*
- use expressions like *absolutely not* to make responses stronger.

Lesson A *Out with the old*

1 Vocabulary in context

A **What are some common gadgets people use these days? Why are they useful? Make a list.**

B CD 2.12 **Read the article from a hiker's blog. Which items in the photos are mentioned?**

The most **rudimentary** instrument that has been widely used for centuries to find direction is the magnetic compass. It was probably invented by the Chinese and was based on the metal lodestone, which had long been admired for its ability to point toward north. **Countless** lives have undoubtedly been saved over the centuries on land and at sea thanks to the compass, which functions equally well in daylight, darkness, or thick fog. Even in our electronic age, magnetic compasses are still being made, and their basic design has not changed for centuries. They are **compact**, **functional**, and **portable**.

Toward the end of the twentieth century, alternatives to the compass were being intensively developed, and **significant** advances were made – thanks to satellite technology. GPS* is now an **integral** part of our daily lives, making moving maps, communicating with smartphones, and offering handheld location devices. It had originally been developed for military purposes, but it soon became part of everyday technology, and **innovative** ways to use GPS – from tracking migrating birds to helping golfers judge their shots – are continually being found through ongoing research. The system has already been incorporated into aircraft and ship design as **standard**, and many other technologies also derive considerable benefit from it.

But what about the **humble** compass? Is it **obsolete** now? Has it been completely forgotten? We'd like to hear your views.

*Global Positioning System

C **Find more formal adjectives in the blog with similar meanings to the words in the chart.**

Vocabulary notebook *See page 61.*

easy-to-carry	portable	creative		useful	
important		out-of-date		usual	
modest		basic		"a lot of"	
necessary		small			

About you

D Pair work **Take turns using the adjectives you found to talk about everyday objects you own.**

"My cell phone is becoming a bit obsolete. It's one of those older flip-phones, but it's functional."

2 **Grammar** Information focus 1

Figure it out

A Write these sentences in the passive. Find similar sentences in the blog to help you, and underline them. Then read the grammar chart.

1. They are continually finding new applications for GPS.
2. All serious hikers were still using the compass until very recently.
3. Has GPS completely replaced the compass?
4. The Chinese had originally developed the compass.

Adverbs within continuous and perfect passive verbs

Grammar extra
See page 152.

The most common position for adverbs is after the first auxiliary verb (*am / is / are / was / were; has / have / had*). Time and attitude adverbs, e.g., *already, always, continually, currently, finally, just, long, since, still; fortunately, sadly,* etc., and the adverbs *also, probably, apparently, reportedly* are usually in this position.
Compasses ***are still being made****. They* ***were continually being improved*** *in the last century.*
GPS ***has already been incorporated*** *into aircraft. It* ***had originally been developed*** *for military use.*

Adverbs that say "how" and "how much" or that describe the participle often go before the participle, e.g., *badly, intensively, seriously, largely, greatly, widely, completely.*
Alternatives to the compass ***were being intensively developed****. It* ***has been widely used****.*

Some adverbs can go in both positions, e.g., *increasingly, previously, largely, originally, initially, continually, generally.*
GPS ***is increasingly being used*** *. . .* OR *GPS* ***is being increasingly used*** *. . .*
It ***has previously been used*** *. . .* OR *It* ***has been previously used*** *. . .*

B Look at these examples of progress. Rewrite the underlined parts of the sentences in the passive. Add the adverbs given – sometimes there are two – and use *by* if necessary.

1. Do you know how memory foam was developed? Well, NASA had developed the material (originally) to improve the safety of aircraft cushions. And now, of course, they are incorporating memory foam (generally) into a whole range of everyday products, like memory-foam beds, which they are using (increasingly) in hospitals. They have saved countless lives (apparently) because foam beds reduce pressure sores when patients are bedridden for long periods of time. And they have improved the lives of these patients (fortunately, greatly).

2. It's interesting when you think about a lot of the things we use in everyday life. Inventors had devised many of them (initially) for other purposes. While they were developing these products (still), no one really thought about spin-offs. Take, for example, smoke detectors. They had produced them (apparently) in the 1970s to help detect toxic gases in the space station. Now they are installing them (increasingly) as standard in newly built homes all over the world.

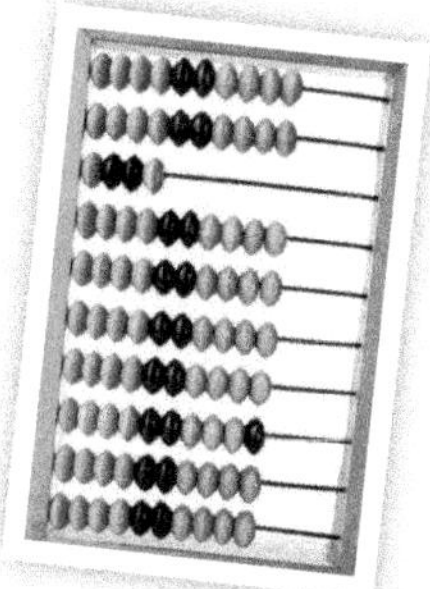

3. The abacus is a tool that we have used (long) for counting and in fact even today, they are using abacuses (currently) in many parts of the world. People think that the Chinese had invented them (originally). And I guess the ones that we are familiar with today were. But they had constructed similar counting boards (already) in Roman times, and they had used them (reportedly, widely) across Europe. Although calculators have overtaken the abacus (largely), it's interesting that they have not made it obsolete (completely).

About you

C Pair work **Read the information again. Then take turns retelling the information. What other examples of progress can you think of?**

Lesson B *What drives us?*

1 Grammar in context

A One kind of progress is when people push the limits of what the human body can do. Why do you think people take on challenges like running marathons or walking across deserts?

"I guess people like to test their limits." "Well, people also do these things to raise funds for charity."

B CD 2.13 **Listen. What dangers did Beaumont face on his expedition?**

AN AMAZING ACHIEVEMENT

In 2008, a 25-year-old Scottish man, Mark Beaumont, set a new record by cycling around the world in 195 days. Although it was an incredible feat, things did not always go smoothly. Pedaling across difficult terrain was often extremely painful. On top of that, his wallet and camera were stolen, and at one point he could easily have been killed in the United States when a motorist drove through a red light. In fact, the whole trip might well have been cut short at several points, owing to sickness, flooded roads, and mechanical problems. Sometimes, when traveling through particularly dangerous regions, he was made to sleep in grim police cells for his own protection.

Beaumont was lucky. He put his life in danger and survived. Others who pursued incredible feats, like climbing Mt. Everest, have died in their attempts. Indeed, the majority of people who have died on Everest were young people with families and partners, so what drove them? They must have known the dangers, so why did they consciously choose to put themselves in harm's way? Some would argue that adventurers like these should not have been permitted to attempt such dangerous expeditions. After all, there are easier – and safer – ways to challenge yourself, raise money for charity, or break world records. Did Mark Beaumont feel that he might not have been given another opportunity to make his mark on the world and pursue his ambition if he hadn't taken this chance?

About you

C Pair work **Answer the questions.**

1. What drives people like Mark Beaumont?
2. What do you think of people who attempt feats like this? Are they adventurous, or reckless and irresponsible?
3. What does *make your mark on the world* mean? How do other people make their marks on the world?
4. If you had an opportunity to follow a dream, what would you do?
5. Would you ever follow a dream that put you in harm's way?

2 Grammar Information focus 2

Figure it out

A **Rewrite the sentences in the passive, starting with the words given. Use similar sentences in the article to help you. Then read the grammar chart.**

1. Something might well have injured Beaumont. Beaumont . . .
2. Something could easily have cut the trip short. The trip . . .
3. They shouldn't have allowed him to do it. He . . .

Past modals and the passive; the verb *make* in the passive

Grammar extra See page 153.

Active sentences	Passive sentences
A motorist ***could*** *easily* ***have killed*** *him.*	*He* ***could*** *easily* ***have been killed*** *(****by*** *a motorist).*
Sickness ***might*** *well* ***have cut short*** *the trip.*	*The trip might well* ***have been cut short*** *(****by*** *sickness).*
They ***shouldn't have permitted*** *him to do it.*	*He* ***shouldn't have been permitted*** *to do it.*
They ***ought (not) to have allowed*** *it.*	*It* ***ought (not) to have been allowed****.*

The verb *make* has a different pattern in the active and passive when it is followed by a verb.
Active: *They made him* ***sleep*** *in police cells.* **Passive:** *He was made* ***to sleep*** *in police cells.*

B **Look at more feats and things people might have said *beforehand*. Rewrite the sentences as what people might have thought *afterward*. Add the adverbs, where given.**

1. **Kristen Ulmer, an extreme skier, skied down the face of Grand Teton, U.S., in 1997.**
   a. An avalanche could bury her alive. *She* could easily have been buried alive by an avalanche. (easily)
   b. They might postpone her attempt due to bad weather. *Her attempt* ______. (well)
   c. They shouldn't encourage her to do it. *She* ______.
2. **Philippe Petit walked a tightrope between the twin towers in New York City in 1974.**
   a. The wind could blow him off. *He* ______. (easily)
   b. They should make him wear a safety harness. *He* ______. (also)
   c. They should never allow him to do it. *He* ______.
3. **Alain Robert got arrested in 2010 after climbing the Lumiere skyscraper in Sydney.**
   a. They shouldn't arrest him, and they shouldn't throw him in jail, either. *He* ______.
   b. He could kill someone if he falls. *Someone* ______. (well)
   c. A company might sponsor him for advertising. They shouldn't give his stunt so much press.
      He ______. *His stunt* ______.

C Pair work **Discuss the feats in this lesson. What else might have happened to the people?**

3 Listening *Kristen Ulmer on extreme skiing*

A CD 2.14 **Listen to a reporter talk about her recent meeting with Kristen Ulmer. Number the topics in the order the speaker mentions them (1–5). There is one topic the interviewer doesn't mention.**

☐ childhood ☐ college ☐ giving up extreme skiing ☐ marriage ☐ travel ☐ film career

B CD 2.15 **Listen again. Circle a, b, or c to complete the sentences.**

1. Kristen started doing dangerous skiing a) as a child. b) in college. c) for movies.
2. As a child, she a) was made to ski. b) was an expert skier. c) enjoyed skiing.
3. Her rule in Asia was a) never discuss skiing. b) tell everyone about skiing. c) look good.
4. In Asia, she might have a) gotten sick. b) lost her life. c) killed someone by accident.
5. While she was filming, she was a) not well known. b) almost killed. c) badly paid.
6. Now she wants to a) transform her performance. b) keep filming. c) coach other athletes.

About you

C Pair work **Would you ever do the kinds of things Kristen has done?**

Lesson C *Just think . . .*

1 Conversation strategy Making a point

A **How has humanity progressed in the last 100 years? Share ideas with the class.**

B CD 2.16 **Listen. What does Alba think about space exploration? How about Jack?**

Alba I see another rocket's just been launched. All this money that's being wasted on going into space. Just think what could have been done with those billions of dollars!

Jack Yes, . . . but one way to look at it is that all kinds of things have been discovered through space exploration.

Alba Like what?

Jack Well, satellite technology, more accurate weather forecasting – they've both come from space programs. And you can't say that we don't need those things.

Alba Absolutely not. But I look at it this way: there are other things we could spend the money on. Don't you think it would have been better spent on things like schools?

Jack Not necessarily. But anyway, things like the space program encourage kids to go into science and engineering. It makes it exciting. I mean, life would be very limited if we never looked beyond our immediate environment.

Alba Well, let me put it another way: maybe we *should* explore space but not till we've made our own world a better place.

Jack Maybe. Maybe not.

C **Notice** how Alba and Jack use expressions like these to make their points. Find the expressions they use in the conversation.

(Let's) put it this way: . . .	***One way to look at it is (that) . . .***
To put it another way: . . .	***Just think.***
Let me put it another way: . . .	***(Just) think about it.***
(I) look at it this way: . . .	

D CD 2.17 **Listen to the rest of Alba and Jack's conversation. Write the expressions you hear.**

Alba Well, ________________ what could have been done to research alternative fuels, for example, if we'd had all those billions of dollars. ________________: there are better things to spend money on.

Jack Yeah, possibly. But ________________: Plenty of countries don't have space programs, but they don't necessarily spend their money on better things.

Alba I'm not sure that's entirely true. I mean, some countries are way ahead in terms of using alternative energies. I mean, ________________: that in itself does more for the planet.

Jack Well, ________________ not only have better technologies been developed, but also new medicines are being discovered. ________________ – all that research that's done in space.

About you **E** Pair work **Practice the whole conversation. Whose opinions do you agree with?**

2 Strategy plus *Absolutely (not), not necessarily*

CD 2.18 You can use ***Absolutely (not)*** or ***Definitely (not)*** to make a *yes* (or *no*) response stronger.

Use ***Probably (not)*** and ***Maybe (not)*** if you do not want to commit strongly to a response.

If you want to say something is not completely or always true, you can say ***Not necessarily***.

About you

Match the statements with the responses. Write the letters a–e. Then practice with a partner. Practice again, giving your own responses.

1. Space exploration is certainly not a waste of money or a waste of time, as some people say. ______
2. Do you think we'll ever discover life on other planets? ______
3. Don't you think we should send humans to Mars, no matter how much it costs? ______
4. Another thing about space programs is they promote international cooperation, which is good. ______
5. Life wouldn't be as exciting if we didn't explore space. ______

a. Probably not. Though there are still plenty of things to explore on earth.
b. Absolutely not. For every dollar spent on space, $8 of economic benefit has reportedly been generated.
c. Definitely. I mean, they've successfully landed a spacecraft there, so why not a human.
d. Not necessarily. I mean, if you want to keep your technology a secret, then it's not good.
e. Maybe. Maybe not. But imagine if we did find other life forms. There'd be a lot of issues to consider.

3 Listening and strategies What's the point of research?

A CD 2.19 **Listen to a conversation. What applications of research do they mention? Check (✓) the topics. There are two extra topics.**

☐ education ☐ social studies ☐ agriculture ☐ climate ☐ medicine

B CD 2.20 **Listen again. What specific research do the speakers mention? Complete the chart.**

Research questions:	**Research question:**
How far can crickets ______________ ?	How do snails ______________ ?
How much ______________ do they do?	**Possible applications of research:**
Possible application of research:	To improve ______________
To ensure ______________	To help people after ______________

About you

C Pair work **Discuss these questions. Give examples or reasons to support your ideas.**

- What research has contributed most to society in the last 10 years?
- Which areas deserve more research? What outcomes would you like to see?
- What subjects do you feel should not be researched? Why?
- Who should pay for research?

Speaking naturally
See page 140.

Lesson D Smart ideas

1 Reading

A Prepare Scan the article. What is the focus of the article? Check (✓) one topic.

☐ How to become an inventor
☐ How to market a new invention
☐ How different inventions come about
☐ Why some inventions fail

B Read for main ideas Read the article. Where do these sentences fit in the article? Write the correct letters in the spaces.

a. There is seemingly no end to the number of inventions we can look forward to in the future.
b. Necessity is the mother of invention – or so the saying goes.
c. The smartphone app is another good example.
d. It is generally believed that inventions are the result of focused effort by inventors seeking specific solutions to specific problems.
e. Clearly, many inventions have come about from a mix of astute observation and inspired thinking.
f. In reality, most people probably will never invent something as world-changing as the steam engine.

INVENTION: INSPIRED THINKING OR ACCIDENTAL DISCOVERY?

1 "To invent, you need a good imagination and a pile of junk," or so Thomas Edison, one of the world's most famous inventors, is quoted as saying. Yet how do successful inventions come about? How have inventions been achieved in the past? What makes something a brilliant invention?

2 ______ Brilliance, however, is not enough, and obviously, hard work and persistence need to follow. James Dyson noticed his vacuum cleaner would frequently clog up and stop picking up dirt. On a visit to a local factory, he observed how dust was removed from the air by large industrial cyclones, and it inspired him to try the same principles on a smaller scale in a vacuum cleaner. He developed over 5,000 prototype designs before finally succeeding with his invention: the first cyclonic bagless vacuum cleaner.

3 ______ Surprisingly, many innovations that have enhanced the efficiency, comfort, and convenience of everyday life have often been discovered by accident. The steam engine, superglue, artificial sweeteners, and synthetic dyes, to name but a few, all came about when their inventors' minds were being applied to quite different problems. If Dr. Percy Spencer had not noticed that a candy bar had melted in his pocket as he was testing microwave radiation for use in radar, the microwave oven may never have been invented.

4 ______ No invention is more true of this proverb than the ice-cream cone. When an ice-cream seller ran out of plates on which to serve his ice cream, he used a rolled-up waffle instead. The ice-cream cone had inadvertently been created, and with great success.

5 ______ Few will have the skills to engineer something like a vacuum cleaner or microwave oven. Even so, when you consider some of the everyday things that have been developed, it's clear that inventions do not have to be complex or life-changing to be hugely successful and incredibly marketable. Tags that label your electrical cords, silly bands for kids, or suitcases with wheels are all examples of inventions that gained huge popularity and left people wondering, "Why didn't I think of that?"

6 ______ By 2011, there were already more than half a million of them, many of which were incredibly simple and straightforward, and many of which had actually been invented by ordinary people and even children. One, nine-year-old Ding Wen from Singapore, invented a drawing app that allows users to draw with their fingers across a touch screen and then shake the device to clear the screen. Another was 14-year-old Robert Nay, an eighth grader from Utah, whose Bubble Ball physics game had reportedly been downloaded more than two million times within two weeks of its launch. What these apps had in common was originality, simplicity, ease of use, and wide demographic appeal.

7 Nevertheless, no matter how inventions come about, whether by sheer brilliance or by a stroke of luck, one thing is clear. ______ What's more, our willingness to adopt them, whether for their effectiveness or simply for our own amusement, means that there will be always be a ready market.

Reading tip
Writers sometimes use a quotation from a famous person or a saying to start and set the theme of an article.

2 **Focus on vocabulary** Adjectives into nouns

A **Complete the sentences below with the noun form of the words given. Use the article to help you. Then match the pictures with the sentences. Write the letters a–d.**

> **Tip**
> Words with the suffixes *-ance, -ence, -ency, -ity, -ness*, and *-ment* are often nouns.

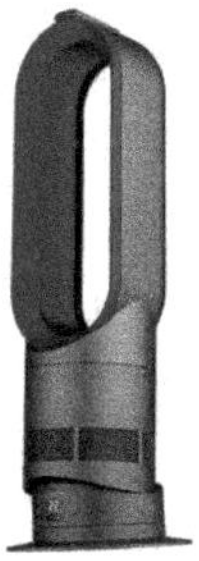
a. a bladeless fan

b. a doodling app

c. mop slippers

d. sticky notes

☐ 1. With the ____________ (willing) of millions to download these, their ____________ (popular) is clear. What apps have you downloaded? How useful are they?

☐ 2. The ____________ (convenient) of this invention is evident, and it certainly wins a prize for ____________ (original). It also provides plenty of ____________ (amuse). But would you really buy something like this?

☐ 3. The sheer ____________ (brilliant) of this invention is clear, and the ____________ (simple) of its design is appealing. It also improves the ____________ (comfortable) of our everyday lives. What other inventions have made life better?

☐ 4. This simple invention certainly improved the ____________ (efficient) of many people's working lives. It's ____________ of use (easy) and ____________ (effective) are part of its winning formula. What other inventions have contributed to a better workplace?

B Pair work **Discuss the questions above. Think of as many ideas as you can.**

3 **Viewpoint** The best ideas . . .

Pair work **Think of ideas for each description below and see if you agree on any of them. Discuss why you made your choices and how the inventions have impacted people's lives.**

Think of . . .

- an invention that improves efficiency in travel.
- an invention that has changed the world.
- an app that is really convenient to have.
- a device that you couldn't live without.
- a simple invention that you wish you had thought of.
- an invention that you'd like to see.
- an app that you would like to develop.

"I guess high-speed rail has really improved the efficiency in travel. The convenience of jumping on a train rather than going to the airport is one reason high-speed trains are so widely used."

> **In conversation . . .**
> You can use *I guess, I think,* or *I suppose* to sound less direct or assertive.

Writing *It is often said . . .*

In this lesson, you . . .

- compare and contrast arguments.
- use *it* clauses + passive.
- avoid errors with *affect* and *effect.*

Task Write an opinion essay.

Some people argue that technological progress is always positive. Others dispute this. What is your view and why?

A Look at a model **Look at the introduction to an essay responding to the question above. Underline the thesis statement. Circle the topics that the student will discuss in the essay.**

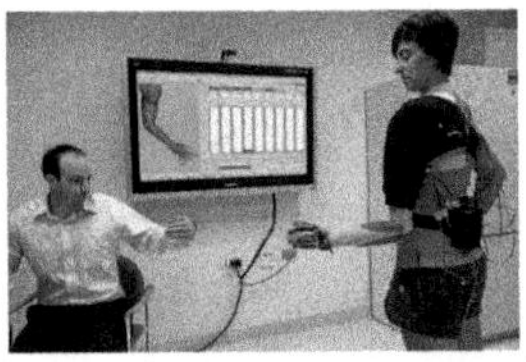

It is often said that technological progress is important and can only have positive or beneficial effects on our lives. Progress, it is argued, especially in the fields of medicine, communications, and infrastructure, has improved the quality of life for human beings. In contrast, others disagree, saying that progress mostly has a negative impact, in particular on the environment. While progress can have both positive and negative effects, I would argue that the positive effects of progress outweigh the negative.

To compare opinions, include:

Introduction – outline the issues and give your view

Opinion 1 with reasons and examples

Opinion 2 with reasons and examples

Conclusion – summarize the arguments and restate your view

B Focus on language **Read the chart. Then rewrite the underlined parts of the sentences below using *it* clauses and the adverbs given.**

_it_ clauses with the passive in academic writing

You can use *it* clauses with the passive to introduce what people say or think. Adverbs like *often, generally, well, widely* emphasize what is commonly said.

***It is often said** that technological progress is important.*

***It is generally accepted** . . . / **widely recognized** . . . / **well known** . . .*

***It has also been reported / shown / suggested** that . . .*

Useful expressions

while / whereas
although
However, . . .
In contrast, . . .
Nevertheless, . . .
On the one / other hand, . . .

1. People accept that progress is inevitable, but we should examine this carefully. (generally)
2. People recognize that progress in industry can cause pollution. (widely) On the other hand, people understand that some industries are making efforts to become "greener." (also)
3. Scientists have shown that life expectancy is increasing as a result of medical advances, although some people suggest that this is only the case in wealthier societies. (also)
4. People know that progress in communications leads to a better-functioning society. (well) Nevertheless, they recognize that privacy and security issues are a growing problem. (widely)
5. People have suggested that technological progress often comes out of military programs. However, people believe that developments like the Internet benefit everyone. (generally)
6. People have reported that so-called industrial progress adversely affects the poor. In contrast, people say that the wealthy become wealthier. (often)

C Write and check **Now write your own opinion essay for the question. Then check for errors. Read a classmate's essay. Do you share the same views?**

Common errors

Do not confuse *affect* and *effect. Affect* is a verb; *effect* is a noun.

*Progress **affects** everyone.* (NOT ~~*Progress effects everyone.*~~)

*Progress has several positive **effects**.* (NOT . . . ~~*several positive affects*~~.)

Vocabulary notebook *Old or ancient?*

Learning tip **Building synonyms**

It's useful to learn more than one way to express basic concepts like *big, small, many, important, good, bad,* etc., especially for formal writing.

bad= inferior, poor

With recent advances in GPS, older versions now seem inferior.

You can be fired for poor performance at work.

Dictionary tip

Your word-processing software probably has a thesaurus to help you find synonyms, but check them in a dictionary before you use them.

A **Choose a synonym from the box for these words. Then complete the example sentences.**

compact countless functional integral obsolete ✓ portable

1. easy to carry = portable ______ We have a portable ______ grill that we barbecue on.
2. useful = ______ Kitchen appliances should be both ______ and attractive.
3. small = ______ With gas prices so high, people are now buying ______ cars.
4. essential = ______ Having ideas is an ______ part of making progress.
5. many, a lot of = ______ There have been ______ inventions that didn't work.
6. out of date = ______ The typewriter has more or less become ______.

B **Write synonyms for these adjectives. Then write a sentence that uses the synonym you came up with.**

1. modest, ordinary = ______ ______
2. creative, new = ______ ______
3. simple, basic = ______ ______
4. important, big = ______ ______
5. usual, not special = ______ ______

C **Word builder These words are all synonyms of one or more words in Exercises A and B. Find their meanings. Then write them next to their synonyms above.**

archaic elementary everyday groundbreaking major practical

D **Focus on vocabulary** **Look back at the article on page 58. Look for the words there and in Exercise 2A on page 59 to help you complete the chart below.**

Adjective	Noun
willing	willingness
popular	
	convenience
original	
amusing	
	brilliance
simple	
	comfort
efficient	
easy	
	effectiveness

Unit 6

Business studies

In Unit 6, you . . .

- talk about business, retail, and threats to companies.
- use relative clauses that begin with pronouns and prepositions.
- use determiners and pronouns like *some, any, other(s), another.*
- persuade people of your views using negative and tag questions.
- *say granted* when someone makes a good point.

Lesson A *A case study*

1 Grammar in context

A **How do people get discounts when they shop? Make a list.**

B CD 2.21 **Read the case study for an online coupon company. How does the business work?**

A CASE STUDY – **Online coupons**

For decades savvy shoppers have been clipping coupons from newspapers and magazines, with which they can save money on everything from groceries to spa treatments. The emergence of the Internet provided a new opportunity to coupon businesses, many of which have been very successful. Then came *Groupon*.

BACKGROUND

Like many start-up companies, *Groupon* was founded by a forward-thinking entrepreneur, in this case, Andrew Mason. As with many such entrepreneurs, some of whom have become overnight multimillionaires, Mason had a deceptively simple idea: attract subscribers to whom you email special deals. These daily promotions give subscribers steep discounts, some of which may exceed 50 percent, on a range of goods and services. The success of any deal depends on the extent to which people sign up. If the number of people who sign up falls short of the target, the deal doesn't go through.

GOALS AND GROWTH

Some of the main goals for the company were to grow their subscriber base in key cities around the world; sell daily deals, which was revolutionary in the coupon business; and create awareness of the brand in national and international markets.

In just three years, it had more than 85 million global customers, all of whom "opt in" to the site. The company also had more than 55,000 merchants from whom deals were sought.

A SUCCESS STORY

Over 90 percent of participating companies, most of which are small businesses, said the *Groupon* promotion attracted new customers, and 87 percent reported increased awareness of their product or service in the community. *Groupon* may not be suitable for every enterprise, but for plenty of small business owners, many of whom struggle to grow, it can be a lifesaver, especially in an uncertain economy. One such small business, a bakery in New York, offered half-price cupcakes. More than 9,000 coupons were purchased, new customers came in, and business spread by word of mouth, all of which has to be good for the bottom line!

C Pair work **Discuss these questions about the article.**

1. What does the writer mean by "savvy" shoppers?
2. Why does the writer refer to the idea behind *Groupon* as "deceptively simple"?
3. Why was *Groupon* "revolutionary" in the coupon business? What did it do?
4. What kinds of successes do small businesses report after using *Groupon*?
5. Why is *Groupon* a "life saver" for some businesses? Why is it good for the "bottom line"?

2 Grammar Adding and modifying information

Figure it out

A How does the writer of the case study express the ideas below? Rewrite each pair of sentences as one sentence. Then read the grammar chart.

1. The emergence of the Internet provided a new opportunity to coupon businesses. Many of these coupon businesses have been very successful.
2. The company also had more than 55,000 merchants. Deals were sought from these merchants.

Pronouns and prepositions in relative clauses

Grammar extra *See page 154.*

You can add pronouns + *of*, e.g., *all of, some of, most of, many of,* etc., or prepositions to relative clauses. Use *whom* for people and *which* for things.

In three years, the company had more than 85 million customers, ***all of whom*** *"opt in" to the site.*
The Internet provided a new opportunity to coupon businesses, ***many of which*** *have been successful.*
Over 90 percent of companies, ***most of which*** *are small businesses, said the promotion attracted customers.*
Mason had an idea: Attract subscribers ***to whom*** *you email special deals.*
Shoppers clip coupons from newspapers, ***with which*** *they can save money.*

Conversation vs. Writing

Relative clauses with pronoun + *of whom / of which* are approximately 10 times more common in academic writing than in conversation.

B Complete the relative clauses from another case study.

1. An entrepreneur needed capital with which______ he was hoping to start his own business.
2. He'd had several ideas, some __________ had potential, but they needed a lot of capital up front.
3. He applied for loans to several banks, all __________ turned down his applications.
4. The friends to __________ he turned for financial help were unable to lend him any money.
5. He talked to several advisors, most __________ advised him not to borrow without a business plan.
6. He finally decided to start a business for __________ he needed very little money – auto detailing. There were several places in his area, most __________ charged very high prices.
7. He sent out flyers for an introductory special offer, to __________ over 100 people replied.
8. Within three weeks, he had serviced cars for 40 customers, many __________ became regular clients.

C Pair work **Take turns retelling details from Exercise B. How much can you remember?**

3 Listening and speaking Too good to be true?

A CD 2.22 **Listen to four consumer experts talk about special promotions. Draw lines to match the goods with the promotions they talk about. There is one extra promotion.**

Goods or services	Promotions
1. electronics	a. "buy one, get one free"
2. restaurants	b. a mail-in rebate promotion
3. clothes	c. "buy one, get one for 50% off"
4. neck massage	d. kids eat free
	e. try it for free

B CD 2.23 **Listen again. What problems does each expert mention? Take notes.**

About you

C Pair work **Which of the promotions in Exercise A do you think work best? Why? Which promotions have you used? What did you buy?**

Speaking naturally *See page 140.*

Lesson B *Bringing in the customers*

1 Vocabulary in context

A How many ways do you shop? What's your favorite way to shop? Take a class vote.

online from a major retailer	online from smaller companies	online at auction sites
in store from a superstore	in store from locally owned stores	other ways?

B CD 2.24 Listen to the podcast. What changes in retail does the speaker predict?

PODCAST LISTEN READ WATCH Share

STATIONS
ABOUT
SUPPORT
LOG IN
SIGN UP

How do you **lure** people into a retail store? Lower prices will **tempt** some people, and some will be **attracted** by special offers, but others know they can probably get what they want cheaper online. In most developed economies, online shopping has grown steadily by about 20 percent a year, while in-store shopping has more or less remained stagnant. To compete, retail stores need to find other ways to **persuade** customers to leave their computers, and **convince** them that there's a better shopping experience in store.

But **coaxing** people to come in and buy is not so easy. Some retailers have found that an effective way of **wooing** customers is to create a store that combines conventional décor and layout with high-tech facilities. Such an environment may look very traditional but also offers facilities like self-service checkouts. Another store might have terminals with self-service ordering for home delivery. Yet another might **entice** customers by creating a social space – a so-called "third place" between work and home – where people can enjoy coffee or read in a relaxed setting without feeling **pressured into** buying things they don't need. Any store that makes people feel at ease will probably generate more business. No store wants to **scare** people **off** or **discourage** them from buying products by creating a cold, unfriendly atmosphere. Some evidence points to the fact that in-store music relaxes customers. Other evidence suggests it can actually irritate people. Equally, no store wants to be so overwhelming that it **puts** people **off** or even **alienates** them. There's a fine balance between **deterring** customers and **drawing** them **in**.

The atmosphere needs to **appeal** to *you*, be like your *home* – not some other unfamiliar place. And since most people don't live in homes the size of aircraft hangars, a store with a small footprint will be less likely to **intimidate.** The superstores of the late twentieth century may well have had their day. Such places were good for browsing a vast range of goods, but we can now browse the whole shopping world online. So in retail, small may prove to be beautiful after all.

Word sort

C Make a chart of verbs in the podcast for attracting people and deterring them. Then use at least six new verbs to tell a partner what attracts you to stores and what deters you.

Attract	Deter
lure	

Vocabulary notebook
See page 71.

2 Grammar Referring to people and things

Figure it out

A Find words in the podcast to replace the ideas in bold. There may be more than one correct answer. Then read the grammar chart.

1. Cheaper prices will attract **certain** people, and **certain people** will find special offers appealing.
2. **Every (and it doesn't matter which)** store that creates a good atmosphere will do well.
3. Lowering prices is one way to attract customers, but stores need to find **additional** ways, too.
4. One store might have nice music. **A different store** might have a restaurant.

some, any, other, others, another

Grammar extra
See page 155.

Some and *any* have "strong" forms. You can use the strong form of *some* to talk about "certain but not all" people or things. The strong form of *any* means "it doesn't matter which."
*Lower prices will tempt **some people**, and **some** will be attracted by special offers.*
***Any** store that makes people feel at ease will probably generate more business.*

Use *other* before a plural or uncountable noun, after *the, your, this, some,* etc.
*Stores need to find **other** ways to attract customers.*
***Other** evidence suggests music can actually irritate people.*
*It needs to be like your home, not **some other** unfamiliar place.*

Others is a pronoun. Don't use it before a noun.
*. . . but **others** know they can probably get what they want cheaper online.* (OR ***other people***)

Common errors

Don't use *another* with a plural noun.
*Retail stores need to find **other ways** to attract customers.* (NOT ~~*another ways*~~)

Use *another* before a singular count noun or as a pronoun to replace a singular count noun.
***Another** store might offer self-service ordering. Yet **another** might create a "third place."*

B Complete the sentences with *some, any, other, others, some other,* and *another*. There may be more than one answer. Then discuss the ideas in pairs. Would they entice you to shop in store?

1. _______ retailers are staying open 24/7 to draw customers in to compete with online stores.
2. _______ retail experts say stores need to attract customers by becoming "idea centers." For example, there are _______ customers who want to see kitchen appliances in a kitchen layout. _______ want to touch products before buying. _______ store that doesn't create an experience may not last.
3. One way stores can compete is to give excellent customer service. _______ way is for stores to provide services you *can't* get online. _______ stores entice people with home-baked cookies that _______ customer can take. _______ stores offer special deals only to in-store customers.
4. There are so many choices for consumers online. Stores could offer a limited selection, but there needs to be _______ choice. _______ suggestion is for retailers to offer shopping advice. Once a retailer has _______ customer in the store, it needs to keep them so they don't go to _______ store.

3 Viewpoint *Online or in store?*

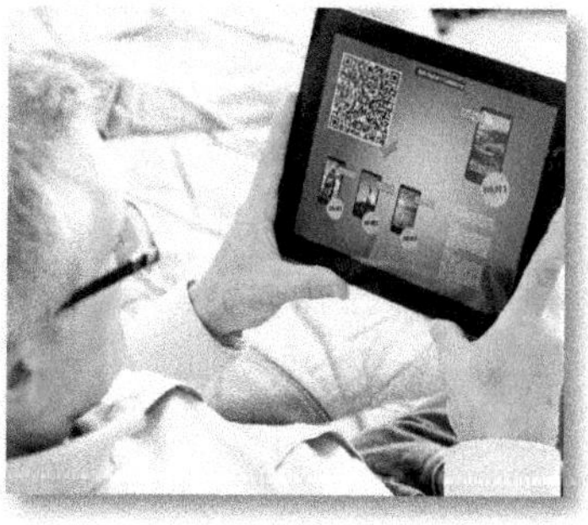

Pair work **Discuss the questions.**

- What are the advantages of shopping online? Are there any disadvantages?
- In what other ways can regular stores compete with online stores?
- What kinds of services do you think shoppers will demand in the future?
- What other changes do you think there will be in the retail business?

In conversation . . .

You can ask *You know what I mean?* to check that others agree with or understand you.

Lesson C *Don't you think . . . ?*

1 Conversation strategy Persuading

A **Do people you know ever boycott, or refuse to patronize a company on principle? Is corporate social responsibility, the idea that companies should be charitable, popular?**

B CD 2.25 **Listen. What is "buycotting"? Do Erkan and Dion agree that it works?**

Erkan Have you heard that expression "to buycott"?

Dion Not sure. What is it?

Erkan It's when you buy a company's products because you support its corporate policies. Like if they support a cause you believe in or if they do business ethically. It's like the opposite of *boycott*.

Dion Oh, right. Does it work? I mean, consumers don't have that much influence, do they?

Erkan But don't you think companies *should* listen to their customers?

Dion Well, to some extent, maybe.

Erkan I think people want businesses to give something back to the community and to have ethical practices. It makes sense for any corporation to do that, doesn't it?

Dion Well, granted the notion of corporate social responsibility is very popular. It's fine in theory. In practice it's more complex than that, isn't it? And in any event, don't companies only do what's good for their bottom line?

C **Notice** how Erkan and Dion use negative questions and tag questions to persuade each other that their opinions are right. Find examples in the conversation.

Don't you think companies **should** ***listen to their customers?***
It makes sense for any corporation, doesn't it?

D **Read more excerpts from the conversation. Rewrite each first question as a negative question, and add a tag question to each response. Then practice with a partner.**

1. ***Erkan*** But do you believe corporate social responsibility is a good thing?
   Dion Yes. But it's not what drives a company, ____________?
2. ***Dion*** And is a company's responsibility to its shareholders, rather than doing good?
   Erkan Well, it's not just a case of either-or. Any business can do both, ____________?
3. ***Erkan*** Do workers feel better when their company stands for something they believe in?
   Dion Perhaps. But many companies are just struggling to survive, ____________?
4. ***Dion*** Are companies having a hard time as it is, without moral pressure from interest groups?
   Erkan Well, it depends. They should still do business ethically, ____________?

About you

E Pair work **Do you agree with any of the opinions in the conversation and Exercise D? Discuss the ideas. Use negative and tag questions to persuade your partner.**

A Don't you believe corporate social responsibility is a good thing? I mean, I do.
B Actually, I do, too. More companies should do business ethically, shouldn't they?

2 Strategy plus *Granted*

CD 2.26 You can use ***granted*** when someone makes a point that is good, but it doesn't change your opinion.

Well, **granted** the notion is very popular . . .

In conversation . . .

Granted often comes near the beginning of what people say, but it can also come in other places.

A CD 2.27 **Match the statements with the responses. Write the letters a–e. Then listen and check.**

1. Don't you think companies often forget that it's their employees that make them successful? ______
2. Manufacturers need to make sure that they're environmentally friendly, don't you think? ______
3. Doesn't the research show that people prefer to buy from socially responsible businesses? ______
4. Don't you believe companies should give a percentage of their profits to charity? ______
5. It's interesting to see the gender and racial balance of people on a company's website. ______

a. They can tell you a lot, granted, but it doesn't mean that they reflect who the company actually employs.
b. Well, granted it's nice to give something back to the community. But you can't make it law, can you?
c. Well, they should, granted. But there's the cost, isn't there? The cost of going green can be prohibitive.
d. People should come first. Granted. But it's often the staff that gets laid off when times are tough.
e. Um, they might *say* that, granted, but when it comes down to it, they probably buy what's cheap.

About you

B Pair work **Discuss the statements above. Do you think any are particularly controversial?**

3 Strategies Big business vs. small business

About you

A **Rewrite the conversations below. Write A's comments using a negative question or a tag question. Add *granted* to B's responses and then complete the idea.**

1. *A* It's better to support small, local businesses. We should all support our neighborhood stores.
   B Well, yeah, it's nice to buy things at small stores and everything. But . . .
2. *A* Big companies typically employ a lot of people. That's a good thing.
   B Yeah, I guess. I mean, they *do* provide a lot of jobs, but . . .
3. *A* The trouble with those big-box stores, you know, the huge superstores, is that they've driven out small-business owners.
   B Well, that can happen. But . . .
4. *A* Small clothing stores tend to give you better personal service. I mean, they have more time for you.
   B Well, it's true. But . . .
5. *A* The biggest advantage of small stores, like small shoe stores, is you can find things that are different. You can also usually find better-quality things.
   B Well, the quality of the products is usually good at small stores. But . . .

B Pair work **What are the advantages of big businesses versus small businesses? Prepare a debate to present to the class.**

A Don't you think that generally it's better to support small, local businesses?
B Not necessarily. I mean, granted, small business is good for a community, but . . .

Lesson D *Organizational threats*

1 Reading

A Prepare **How might a company "leak" or lose electronic data (information)? Make a list.**

B Read for main ideas **Read the article. How many of your ideas are mentioned? What types of data leakage can you find? What are the reasons for it?**

Data leakage - are you protected?

1 Like any company, your business is no doubt one in which technology is widely used. Online banking, sales, networked collaboration, and communication are central to your operation, and your IT professionals carefully safeguard your electronic data. But how secure is that data? You might well have software that protects you from the external threats of hacking and industrial espionage, but are you overlooking another threat that's closer to home?

2 You probably encourage your staff to take work home. With laptops, portable storage devices, and smartphones, it's easy for employees to finish off that report at night or reply to email on the train to work. Thanks to technology, you have a productive workforce that works for you during off hours. However, this means your confidential company data is out "in the open," outside of your premises. It's less secure and is vulnerable to misuse and theft. And you don't need reminding that the loss or leaking of sensitive financial data, strategic plans, and intellectual property could not only cost your company its competitive edge but could ruin it completely.

THE ENEMY WITHIN?

3 Research* commissioned by Cisco® and carried out by InsightExpress in 10 countries estimated that within a two-year period, over 250 million confidential records were either lost or stolen. The research also revealed the extent to which employee behavior, both innocent and malicious, can put company data at risk. While insiders were responsible for 21 percent of electronic crimes – as opposed to 58 percent for outsiders – the companies surveyed estimated that 33 percent of insider crimes were costly or damaging.

REASONS FOR DATA LEAKAGE

4 Yet, even without crime, there are many more mundane reasons for data leakage. The report paints a worrisome picture of employee behaviors, among which is using company computers to access personal email. Even though many employers do not allow this, almost 80 percent of employees do it, over 60 percent of whom do it at least once a day. Unauthorized applications for email, online banking, or shopping can put your computers at risk from theft or viruses from malicious sites.

5 Other common behaviors are when employees knowingly bypass or change security settings to access sites for personal use and also when they fail to use passwords or log off correctly. According to the report, one-third of employees leave their computers on without logging off when they leave their desks, including overnight, and a fifth leave logon information in insecure places, often next to their computers.

6 Remote working also causes problems if employees transfer or copy data from company computers to home computers, to which others may have access and many of which may not have the same level of security. Computers and storage devices can be lost or stolen when used in public, and the practice of discussing sensitive company information in public, where others can overhear, is widespread. Incredibly, 25 percent of employees admit to sharing such information with friends, family, and strangers.

WHAT'S TO BE DONE?

7 The practices described above may not even be considered problematic by employees, many of whom would see their actions as entirely legitimate. Training and insistence upon the observance of security protocol is one way to handle it.

Continued on the next page …

* http://www.cisco.com/en/US/solutions/collateral/ns170/ns896/ns895/white_paper_c11-499060.html

C Understanding inference **Answer the questions about the article. Then compare with a partner.**

1. Who is the article written for? What is it trying to do? Why does the title ask that question?
2. What does the writer mean by "... another threat that's closer to home"?
3. What do 60 percent of employees do every day?
4. What point is the writer trying to make by quoting the percentages of insider crime?
5. What does the writer think about employees sharing information outside the company?
6. Why might employees think their use of a company computer is "legitimate"?

About you

D React **What did you read in the article that surprised you about data leakage? Will the information make you change any of your behaviors in the future?**

2 Focus on vocabulary Adjectives

A **Find the words below in the article. Can you figure out their meanings? Then match them to the words in the second column with a similar meaning. Write the letters a–g.**

1. secure (para. 1) and insecure (para. 5) _____
2. confidential and sensitive (para. 2) _____
3. vulnerable (para. 2) _____
4. malicious (para. 3) _____
5. mundane (para. 4) _____
6. widespread (para. 6) _____
7. legitimate (para. 7) _____

a. open to attack
b. harmful
c. everyday, unexciting
d. acceptable
e. common, affecting many people or places
f. private and not to be discussed openly
g. safe and unsafe

About you

B Pair work **Use the adjectives above to rephrase the questions. Then discuss with a partner.**

- What are acceptable uses of an employer's computer? What's not acceptable?
- How common do you think hacking is these days?
- Are you personally open to attack by harmful software?
- How do you keep your private information safe, especially online?
- Do you ever feel that really private information about you is unsafe online?

3 Listening and speaking The top threats

A CD 2.28 **Look at these threats to organizations. Guess the top five threats companies fear. Then listen to an interview and check your guesses. Number the threats 1–5.**

- ☐ unplanned IT and telecom outages
- ☐ industrial disputes
- ☐ malicious software and other cyber attacks
- ☐ interruption to utility supplies
- ☐ adverse weather
- ☐ loss of personnel talent
- ☐ loss or theft of confidential information
- ☐ new laws or regulations

B CD 2.29 **Listen again. In what specific way can each threat impact a business? Write notes on a separate piece of paper.**

C Pair work **How could the other threats described in Exercise A disrupt business? What other threats might organizations face?**

Writing *It can occur in any company.*

In this lesson, you . . .

- write about causes of and solutions to a problem.
- use modals to avoid being too assertive.
- avoid errors with *can* and *could*.

Task **Write a report on data security.**
Write a report for your boss, describing the possible causes of data leakage. Propose some potential solutions in your workplace.

A Look at a model **Brainstorm some ideas about the causes of and solutions to data leakage for a report. Then look at the extracts from a report below. Does it include any of your ideas?**

Leakage of sensitive data is a serious problem, which can occur in any company for a number of reasons. One reason may be the fact that employees take work outside of the office on portable devices. Some of these devices might be shared with other people or may not be as secure as company computers. Second, employees can access their personal email and other websites from work computers and they may fail to observe security procedures when doing so. This could allow malicious software to attack company servers. Another cause of data leakage is thought to be . . .

All of the above factors can cause data leakage, which could potentially damage the company's profits and image. To prevent data leakage, a number of security measures should be employed, many of which are simple to implement.
1. As a company, we need to control what data leaves the building. It would be advisable not to allow employees to take work home.
2. We could also enforce the rules on using private computers.
. . .

B Focus on language **Read the chart and underline the modal verbs in Exercise A.**

Using modal verbs in writing

You can use modals to avoid being too assertive in describing situations.
These factors ***can*** *cause data leakage.* (= they can and do)
Some devices ***might / may / could*** *be shared with others.* (it is possible)

You can also use modals to make polite recommendations.
It ***would*** *be advisable not to allow employees to take work home.*
We ***could*** *also enforce the rules on using private computers.*

Describing cause

One reason for this might be . . .
A possible cause could be . . .
This may be a result of . . .
It can be caused by . . .

C **Rewrite the underlined parts of each sentence below using the modal verbs given.**

1. Security is improved if procedures are in place. Data leakage is a result of poor security. (can, may)
2. A possible cause of data leakage is that employees don't realize that they should not discuss work with friends and family. One reason for this is a lack of training. (could, may, might)
3. Data leakage is also caused by employees' use of instant-messaging programs. (might)
4. Certain Internet sites are infected by viruses, so it is advisable to limit access to them. (may, would)
5. Employees' laptops infect company computers, which causes data loss. (might, may)
6. One possible solution is to check employees' devices on a regular basis for malware. (could)

D Write and check **Write the report on data leakage in the task above. Then check for errors.**

Common errors

Do not use *could* for things which in fact do happen.
Employees can access their personal email. = They do this, we know.
(NOT ~~*Employees could access*~~ *. . .*, except in sentences like this:
Employees could access their email if we allowed it. = It would be possible.)

Vocabulary notebook *It's tempting.*

Learning tip Word families

When you learn a new verb, use a dictionary to help you find other words in the same family. Write them in a chart. *Note*: Some words are only or mostly used as verbs and don't have other forms.

Verb	Noun	Adjective	Mostly as verb
tempt	temptation	tempting	coax

A **Complete the charts with verbs from the podcast on page 64. Then add nouns and adjectives from the same word family to the chart on the left.**

Verb	Noun	Adjective(s)
	conviction (= a belief)	
deter		
		discouraging / discouraged
persuade		
	pressure	

Mostly used as verbs
put off
scare off
woo

B **Make a chart with these verbs.**

alienate   appeal   attract   coax   draw in   entice   intimidate   lure

C Word builder **Find the meaning of these verbs. Are they verbs that mean "attract" or verbs that mean "deter"?**

dissuade   induce   prompt   unnerve   urge

D Focus on vocabulary **Which of the adjectives below have other forms in the same family with the same meaning? What are they? Write them in the chart. Use Exercise 2A on page 69 to help you.**

	Adjectives	Nouns	Adverbs
1.	secure / insecure		
2.	confidential		
3.	sensitive		
4.	vulnerable		
5.	malicious		
6.	mundane		
7.	widespread		
8.	legitimate		

Checkpoint 2 *Units 4–6*

1 Breaking records – an ongoing achievement

A Complete the passive verbs, adding the adverbs given. There may be more than one word order. Then replace the words in bold with synonyms, changing *a* to *an* if necessary.

significant

In 1954, Roger Bannister achieved a **big** milestone: he ran a mile in under four minutes. This was something that had ______________ (see, previously) as almost impossible, though **a lot of** people had tried. The four-minute barrier has ______________ (break, since) numerous times and is now the **normal** time for most medium-distance runners. In fact, records in track are ______________ (achieve, still) today, largely thanks to **creative, new** technology. Technology has ______________ (use, widely) to enhance performance in the sport. Running shoes are ______________ (improve, continually) and are far different from the **basic** rubber-soled shoes of the 1950s, which are now **out of date**. Clothing is much more **useful**, too. Even the **ordinary** T-shirt has ______________ (redesign, completely) so that it removes sweat from an athlete's body. In addition, **easy-to-carry** and **small** devices, such as GPS watches, can monitor heart rate, etc., and are now a **necessary** part of tracking a runner's performance. Further advances in sports technology are ______________ (make, currently). It's a **continuing** process, and it may only be a matter of time before we see the headline, "The three-minute-mile barrier has ______________ (shatter, finally)."

B Pair work **Discuss each of the topics below about sports and athletics today. Use *In any case* to make your argument stronger and *In any event* to reach your final conclusion.**

- use of performance-enhancing drugs
- high salaries that some athletes receive
- training children from an early age to compete
- use of technology to improve performance

2 They could easily have become extinct.

A Unscramble the underlined verb phrases. Then complete the relative clauses.

1. In the last few years, the tiger been have could wiped off easily the planet by poachers. But the extinction of tigers prevented may been have well by innovative programs, some ______________ focus on preserving tiger habitats. How else can we protect endangered species?
2. When some endangered species were first brought into captivity, there were critics, many ______________ believed that breeding endangered animals in captivity have not been should permitted. Although some programs failed well might have, many didn't. What is your view on keeping animals in captivity?
3. News reports have detailed specific cases of wild animals attacking their trainers, all ______________ suffered severe injuries, which killed have could easily them. Other reports highlight how wild animals, many______________ are losing their habitats, encroach into neighborhoods and are shot. In other cases, animals have been to perform made in jobs and entertainment. What is your response to this treatment of animals? How can people protest, and to______________ should they send their complaints?

B Pair work **Discuss the questions above. Use expressions like *Apart from anything else, What's more,* etc., to add and focus on new ideas. Use *granted* if your partner makes a good point that doesn't change your opinion.**

"Well, it's important to educate people about tigers in addition to preserving their habitats."

3 That's the business!

A Read the headline. Then write as many words as you can to replace *woo* and *deterred*.

Stores use smart tactics to **woo** customers. Don't be **deterred**! But be careful.

attract intimidate

B Complete the sentences. Use a form of the future perfect of the verbs given, if possible, or the simple present if not. More than one form may be correct. Then add the words from the box.

another	another	any	other	others	some	some	some

"Black Friday" is the start of the holiday shopping season. By the time Black Friday ____________ (arrive), retailers need to be ready. Most stores ____________ (prepare) for the sales for weeks. They ____________ (stock) their shelves with goods at low prices. When the doors ____________ (open), ____________ store that is not ready may end up not making a profit for the whole year. Stores ____________ (advertise) their deals for days. ____________ reduce prices by 50 percent. ____________ take up to 75 percent off. By the time the doors open, ____________ customers ____________ (wait) in line for several hours. ____________ shoppers ____________ (camp out) for more than 24 hours to get the best deals. However, not all are genuine. ____________ stores advertise deals, but there's only one item at this price. ____________ tactic is to sell old goods. ____________ is to sell products made just for the sale. By the time stores close, they ____________ (serve) millions of customers. They ____________ (take in) millions of dollars in revenue, and no doubt some customers ____________ (spend) more than they intended to.

C Rewrite each comment in two ways: (1) as a negative question; (2) by adding a tag question. Then discuss the ideas with a partner. Use strong responses and expressions like *Just think* and *Let's put it this way* to make your point.

1. It's crazy to camp out all night until a store opens.
2. It makes sense for stores to offer big discounts.
3. People buy things just because they're on sale.
4. Sales are just a clever marketing tool.

A Don't you think it's crazy to camp out all night until a store opens?
B Oh, absolutely not! Just think: you can get some really great deals.

4 Surviving it all

Complete the prepositional phrases. Then choose the correct words to complete the article.

Bald eagles are not actually bald, which may not be in ____________ with most people's expectations. ____________ from being the national symbol of the United States, it is a protected species. Northern eagles migrate but return to the same breeding **ground / young** year after year and **mate / hibernate** for life. They often build their **nests / burrows** near water on ____________ of the fact that they feed mostly on fish. They **dig / lay** between one and three eggs, which **mate / hatch** after 35 days. The eagles sit on the nest to **keep / store** the eggs warm and also to prevent them being attacked by **predators / reserves** such as squirrels. The parents initially **hatch / raise** the young in the nest, but once the chicks have feathers, the parents stop **feeding / breeding** them and they may go up ____________ several days without eating. Far ____________ being neglectful, the parents are simply encouraging the chicks to leave the nest and learn to fly. Once out of their nests, the chicks are fed by the parents to build up their fat **reserves / habits** and are taught to hunt so they can **survive / migrate** the winter months. Bald eagles don't **store / build up** food or **hibernate / breed**, and they often hunt other birds. Their presence in an area can be unwelcome ____________ to the fact that they can destroy other birds' **colonies / grounds**.

Unit 1, Lesson C Stressing auxiliaries for emphasis

People often add the stressed auxiliary verbs *do, does, did,* or stress the full form of the auxiliary verbs with *be* or *have* (e.g., *am, was, have,* and *had*) to emphasize an idea.

*I'm not surprised John didn't come to the party, but I **am** surprised he didn't call! I mean, I **had** asked him to let me know if he couldn't come, so I really **did** think he would call me.*

A **Read and listen to the information above. Repeat the example sentences.**

B **Read the conversation. Rewrite the phrases in bold to emphasize the speakers' ideas. Then listen, check, and repeat.**

I do know

A **I know** computers help people learn, but **I think** they often make it difficult to concentrate.
B Well, at one point **I worried** that using computers in class was a mistake, but now I don't.
A Yeah, no. I mean, **it's been shown** that math students learn algebra faster on a computer.
B And **it's** true that students often pay more attention to a good computer program. . . .
A But **I've noticed** that students spend a lot of time doing other things instead of studying.
B Yeah, **I'd hoped** that wouldn't happen, but there are lots of distractions on the Internet.

About you **C** Pair work **Practice the conversation. Then discuss the ideas. Which do you agree with?**

Unit 2, Lesson A Stress in noun phrases

Notice the stress in these noun phrases. The primary stress is on a word after the noun or pronoun. The main noun or pronoun gets the secondary stress.

information online	*attitudes toward privacy*	*information considered private*
people on social networks	*ads requesting private information*	*something to worry about*

A **Read and listen to the information above. Repeat the phrases.**

B **Listen. In the bold phrases, underline the syllable with the secondary stress and circle the syllable with the primary stress. Then listen, check, and repeat.**

1. I often feel that **attitudes toward privacy** are changing for the worse. It seems like **information once considered private** is now shared freely on social networks.
2. I ran into a problem after checking out some **products on the Internet**. On every website I went to, I got all these **ads for similar products**.
3. Someone hacked into my email, probably because I used a **password based on my birthdate**. Now when I choose passwords, I never choose **anything obvious**.
4. I have maximum privacy settings on my social networks so my boss won't see the **photos posted by my friends**. That really is **something to think about**.

About you **C** Pair work **Have you or has anyone you know had these problems? Tell your partner.**

Unit 3, Lesson C Stress in expressions of contrast

Notice which words are stressed in these expressions introducing a contrasting view.

It's important to get a college degree, ***but even then****, you won't necessarily find a job.*
Having said that, though*, your chances are better if you finish college.*

There's a lot of competition for jobs these days. ***But then again****, there always has been.*
Even so*, the competition is probably more intense now than ever.*

A **Read and listen to the information above. Repeat the example sentences.**

B **Listen. Circle the stressed word in each bold expression. Then listen, check, and repeat.**

1. I think you should attend the best college that accepts you. **Having said that, though**, you need to make sure you can afford the housing and tuition costs.
2. I think it's great that people have a shorter workweek than they used to. **But then again**, many people now work two jobs in order to earn enough money to live on.
3. More people are working overtime, **but even then**, many have a hard time paying their bills.
4. I think it's good that people are getting married later, when they're more mature. **But even so**, the divorce rate doesn't seem to be going down.
5. There *is* competition for jobs. **Having said that**, there aren't enough candidates for some jobs.

About you **C** Pair work **Discuss the comments. Which views do you agree with?**

Unit 4, Lesson C Stress in adding expressions

Notice which words are stressed in these expressions that add information.

Overfishing decreases the fish population, ***not to mention*** *that many fish are killed by pollution.*

On top of that*, fish consumption continues to increase every year.*

What's more*, no one seems interested in finding a solution to the problem.*

In any case*, someday people will have to consume less fish, or there won't be any left to eat.*

A **Read and listen to the information above. Repeat the example sentences.**

B **Listen to these conversations. Circle the stressed word in each bold expression. Then listen, check, and repeat.**

1. *A* No one seems to agree on the causes of global warming. **What's more**, they don't agree on any solutions, either.
   B I suppose it's hard to identify the causes, but **in any event**, we need to do something.
   A I agree. I mean, we need to prepare for higher temperatures, **not to mention** extreme weather events like hurricanes. And **on top of that**, there's rising sea levels.
2. *A* The world uses way too much oil, and **what's more**, demand is increasing every year.
   B Yeah. **Not to mention** the fact that the supply of oil is decreasing pretty quickly.
   A And **on top of that**, people aren't trying very hard to develop different energy sources.
   B You're right. **In any case**, we'll need to do something soon. We're running out of oil.

About you **C** Pair work **Practice the conversations. Then discuss the issues. What's your view?**

Unit 5, Lesson C Stress in expressions

Notice that in these expressions, which introduce different perspectives on an issue, the primary stress is on the determiners, and the secondary stress is on the verbs.

■ ▪
One way to look at it *is that space exploration is a good investment.*

▪ ■
I don't really agree. ***Let me put it this way****: If money's limited, you need to set priorities.*

▪ ■
To put it another way*: As long as people are hungry, we can't waste money on space.*

A **Read and listen to the information above. Repeat the example sentences.**

B **Listen to these conversations. In the bold expressions, circle the primary stress and underline the secondary stress. Then listen, check, and repeat.**

1. *A* I think we need to cut back on government spending, including education.
   B Well, yes, but **look at it this way**: Education is the key to our children's future.
2. *A* I think we spend too much on infrastructure – you know, highways, bridges, and things.
   B Well, **one way to look at it is** investing in infrastructure creates jobs, which we need. **To put it another way**, it makes the economy grow.
3. *A* They should eliminate taxes on gasoline. Gas costs too much these days.
   B Well, I'm not too sure. **Let me put it this way**: Taxes help lower consumption. Or **to look at it another way**, if we don't tax gas, consumption rises and it'll cost more.

About you **C** Pair work **Practice the conversations. Then discuss the ideas. Who do you agree with, Speaker A or Speaker B?**

Unit 6, Lesson A Prepositions in relative clauses

Notice how the prepositions before the relative pronouns are reduced. Notice also which word has the primary stress in each phrase.

■ ▪
Online coupons bring in new customers, ***some of whom*** *become regular customers later on.*

■ ▪
These coupons generate income for gyms, ***many of which*** *have equipment that isn't used for long periods during the day.*

A **Read and listen to the information above. Repeat the example sentences.**

B **Listen and repeat these sentences. Pay particular attention to the weak forms of the prepositions and the stressed words in the bold expressions.**

1. Online coupons don't always work for small restaurants, **most of which** have low profits.
2. The steep discounts, **some of which** attract lots of customers, often don't continue long term.
3. Restaurants get paid a low fee for their meals, **half of which** goes to the coupon website.
4. Coupons attract particular types of people, **many of whom** never return for a full-price meal.
5. Often a restaurant's regular customers, **all of whom** pay full price, get annoyed that others are getting better deals.

About you **C** Pair work **Discuss the ideas in the sentences. Which do you agree with?**

1 More on auxiliary verbs to avoid repetition

- You can use auxiliary verbs to avoid repetition of these verb tenses and forms.

Simple present or past	*I don't often take risks, but my best friend* ***does*** *all the time.*
Present or past continuous	*I was hoping to graduate last year. One of my friends* ***was,*** *too.*
Present perfect (or continuous)	*I've been thinking about settling down, but my friends* ***haven't****.*
Past perfect (or continuous)	*I'd never had straight A's till this year, though my friends all* ***had****.*
Modal verbs	*My dad can't understand why I want to travel, but my mom* ***can****.*

Use auxiliary and modal verbs to complete what these people say about the different topics. Use the same tense and form as the first verb.

1. *Work:* Well, I was trying to get a job in TV. Actually, I know a couple of other people who ________, too. But I'm finding it difficult to get *any* job, as many people ________ these days.
2. *Family:* I've never really thought about starting a family, and I know my husband ________ either. I'm getting so involved in my career at the moment, as we all ________, I guess.
3. *Relationships:* I hadn't really met anyone serious until now, though a couple of my friends ________. I mean, I can really imagine getting married now – I just hope my girlfriend ________!
4. *Social life:* It's funny. Some of my friends are going to parties still, but I ________. I'm not interested. I want to do other things with my life now. I think my closest friend ________, too.
5. *Hobbies:* I haven't had much time to do anything, but my wife ________. She's been learning how to edit videos. I don't often use my computer now; well, I ________ a bit but not a lot.
6. *Travel:* My sister and I went to Italy last fall. I hadn't gone overseas before that, and she ________, either. We had a fabulous time. Now I want to go away again – and my sister ________, too.

2 *too, either, so, neither,* and *(to) do so*

- You can use auxiliaries with *too, either, so,* and *neither* to show similarity. After *so* and *neither,* change the order of the auxiliary and subject.
  I am saving for a trip, and ***my best friend is, too****.* OR *. . . and* ***so is my best friend****.*
  She doesn't enjoy her work, and ***I don't, either****.* OR *. . . and* ***neither do I****.*
  She can't afford to go away next year, and ***I can't, either****.* OR *. . . and* ***neither can I****.*
- Use (*to*) *do so* to avoid repeating a verb + object or complement.
  Learning to play sports has given me confidence and will ***continue to do so*** *for many years.*
  Many people want to buy their own home but are not in a ***position to do so****.*
  A lot of people want to publish novels but are ***unable to do so****.*
  Anyone who wishes to take a career break ***can do so*** *if they plan it carefully.*

Complete the bold phrases with an auxiliary and the sentences with *(to) do so.* Then write another way to state the bold phrases using *so* or *neither*.

1. To get ahead in your career, you often have to move to another city. I don't really want to uproot my family, and **my wife** ________**, either**, but if necessary, we'll ________.
2. A friend asked me to go to a debate club last year with him, and you know, I was happy ________. And actually, I'm glad I did. I can speak much more confidently now, and **my friend** ________**, too.**
3. It's easier than ever now to take a year off before college if you can ________.
4. My friend's thinking of studying in Paris. **I** ________**, too**, if I can get the money ________.
5. I've always wanted to go on a cycling tour, but I've never had the time ________. But finally my sisters and I are planning to go next spring. I'm looking forward to it, and **my sisters** ________**, too.**

1 More on using *to* to avoid repeating verb phrases

- You can use *to* to avoid repeating an infinitive verb phrase when it is clear what you mean. Use *to* after *choose, deserve, expect, hate, hope, like, mean, intend, need, prefer, want, 'd like.*
  I've never written a journal. I keep meaning ***to****. / But I hope* ***to****. / I'd prefer* ***not to****.*
- You don't need *to* after *agree, ask, promise, forget, try,* or after *want, like, wish* in *if* clauses.
  "I want to get my novel published. I've tried ***(to)*** *but can't." "I'll look at it if you* ***want / like / wish****."*
- When you use *be* in the first clause, including in the passive, use *to be* in the second clause.
  My parents ***aren't*** *interested in poetry, and they've never pretended* ***to be****.*
  In college, I ***was asked*** *to enter a short-story contest, though I didn't expect* ***to be****.*

Complete the comments with *to* or *to be*. Write parentheses where *to* is not needed.

1. A classmate asked me to comment on her poems. Well, I promised __(to)__, and I really tried ________. But they were really bad. After a month, she asked, "Did you read them?" I said, "Sorry, I forgot ________."
2. My friend has entered a few writing contests. She's never won, though she always expects ________.
3. I'd love to see a Shakespeare play in English. I've always wanted ________, and I intend ________ one day.
4. I was voted the best fiction writer in high school, though I didn't deserve ________.
5. You can borrow my e-reader if you want ________. I lost some books off it. I didn't mean ________, but . . .
6. I'm just not very good at writing, and I'll never hope ________, really. I'll stick to math!
7. My sister wants to work in publishing. Well, she hopes ________.
8. I think I'm going to have to play the lead role in the school play, but I'd prefer not ________.

2 More on *one / ones* to avoid repeating countable nouns

- You need to use *one / ones* after *the, the only, the main, every,* and after adjectives.
  I read six plays last week – a ***long one*** *and five* ***short ones****.* ***The one*** *I liked best was the* ***long one****.*
- You don't need *one / ones* after *which,* superlatives, *this, that, either, neither, another, the other.*
  "Can I borrow a book?" "Sure. ***Which (one)*** *do you want? You can take* ***this (one)*** *or* ***that (one)****."*
- Don't use *one / ones* after *these, those, my, your, Dan's,* etc., *some, any, both,* or numbers.
  *"****Both (books)*** *are good. They're both* ***mine****."* (NOT . . . ~~*my ones*~~.)
- In formal English, especially writing, use *that / those* or a possessive instead of the *one / ones.*
  Keats's poems are better than ***those of Byron / Byron's****.*

Common errors

Notice the spelling of *ones.*
I love books. The ***ones*** *I like best are . . .*
(NOT . . . ~~*once / one's I like*~~)

Replace the underlined words with *one / ones* if possible or make other changes to avoid repeating.

1. *A* Can I take a look at one of your magazines? I mean, these <u>magazines</u> on your desk.
   B Sure. Which <u>magazine</u> do you want to read?
   A Either <u>magazine</u>. Oh, actually, I'll take a look at that <u>magazine</u>. It's an expensive <u>magazine</u>.
   B Actually, that's the only <u>magazine</u> worth reading. It's the <u>magazine</u> I prefer, anyway. The other <u>magazine</u> doesn't have very many interesting articles.
2. *A* My literature classes are fun. Are your <u>literature classes</u>? I have three <u>literature classes</u> a week.
   B Well, Mrs. Brown's classes are the hardest <u>classes</u>. She said in her lecture last week, "My class is more demanding than Mr. Smith's <u>class</u>." And honestly, the homework is hard. I mean, listen to this: "The works of J.K. Rowling are as important as <u>the works</u> of Shakespeare. Discuss."

1 Adjectives after nouns

- Adjectives usually come before nouns, but these adjectives often come after nouns:
  available, possible, concerned, responsible, involved, necessary, extra.
  Cybercrime is a problem, and the people ***responsible / involved*** *should be punished.*
  There are various antivirus programs ***available****.*
  Look for the easiest solution ***possible****.*
- Adjectives come after nouns in measurements and after indefinite pronouns.
  Social media sites are only about a ***decade old****.*
  There's ***nothing unusual*** *about getting spam mail.*
  Anyone interested *in protecting themselves from cybercrime should talk to an expert.*
- Adjectives with complements come after nouns.
  One action ***worth taking*** *is changing your password regularly.*
  Websites ***full of personal data*** *can be targets for identity thieves.*

Unscramble the sentences. Put the adjectives after the nouns.

1. a great deal of / personal information / Some people / have / available online
   Some people have a great deal of personal information available online.
2. with doing this / wrong / don't think / They / there's anything
3. your personal data / any means / eager to get / However, hackers / will try / possible
4. responsible for hacking / It can be / the people / to find / difficult
5. may "lose" / People / confidential information / what hackers / are doing / unaware of
6. The victims / problems with / concerned / their credit / may end up having
7. the steps / You need to / take / necessary / to protect yourself

2 Negative phrases after nouns

- Phrases that come after nouns can be negative. You can add *not* after the noun.
  Some information can be hidden from people ***not in your group of "friends."***
  Individuals ***not willing to give personal information*** *shouldn't have to do so.*
  Emails ***not to trust*** *often have the subject "Hi."*
  Credit card numbers are one example of the kind of data ***not to be shared****.*
  Social networking sites can be a mystery to anyone ***not belonging to one****.*
  Any computer ***not protected by antivirus software*** *is vulnerable.*

A Complete the sentences using the words given. Sometimes there is more than one answer.

1. These days anyone________ (not / wish) to have their information online may find it impossible.
2. Computers ________ (not / protect) by antivirus software are unsafe.
3. If you think you've been hacked, there are some warning signs ________ (not / ignore).
4. There are some basic rules for first-time users ________ (not / familiar) with social networks.
5. Your phone number is one example of information ________ (not / post).
6. Don't allow people ________ (not / in your contacts list) to read your profile.
7. Another thing ________ (not / do) is to post photos of yourself doing silly things.
8. Remember that your problems at work are a subject ________ (not / discuss) on social media sites.
9. Online ads ________ (not / click) on are the ones that say you won a prize.

About you

B Choose a sentence from Exercise A that you agree with. Explain why.

I agree. It's almost impossible for people not wishing to have their information online to stop it from happening. Every time you sign up to a website you have to give personal information.

1 More on two-part conjunctions

- You can use two-part conjunctions to combine nouns, adjectives, and verbs.

Nouns	*My TV can play **either DVDs or** Internet **movies**.* ***Both the mouse and the keyboard** are wireless.* *My friend has **neither a TV nor a computer** in her home.* *The kitchen has **not only a self-cleaning oven but also a robot** that cleans the floors.*
Adjectives	*Some high-tech products are **either very expensive or very complicated**.* *Housework is **both boring and tiring**.* *Housecleaning with modern appliances is **neither difficult nor time-consuming**.* *Using a microwave to cook is **not only simple but also fast**.*
Verbs	*You can **either raise or lower** all the blinds with a remote control.* *My alarm clock **both flashes** lights **and sounds** an alarm to wake me up.* *Older cell phones **neither play** music **nor take** pictures.* *I'd like a robot that **not only cleans** the house **but also cooks** the meals.*

Common errors

Don't use *neither . . . nor* when you have already used a negative verb. Use *either . . . or.*
*We do not have **either** a dishwasher **or** a washing machine.* (NOT ~~*We do not have neither a*~~ *. . .*)

If you use a modal verb, put it before the first conjunction.
*My TV **can either** stream movies **or** play DVDs.* (NOT *My TV* ~~*either can stream*~~ *. . .*)

Rewrite the sentences using the two-part conjunctions in parentheses.

1. Many features in high-tech homes are convenient. They are innovative. (both . . . and)
   Many features in high-tech homes are both convenient and innovative.
2. In high-tech homes, one control manages temperature. It manages lighting. (both . . . and)
3. Remote computers can control the central systems. Smartphones can control them. (either . . . or)
4. In new, high-tech homes, cooking is simpler. It is more efficient. (not only . . . but also)
5. Refrigerators list their contents. They suggest recipes for the foods available. (not only . . . but also)
6. Cookbooks won't be needed anymore. Recipe cards won't be needed anymore. (neither . . . nor)
7. A computer displays the recipes on your kitchen counter. It reads the recipes aloud. (both . . . and)

2 Two-part conjunctions with phrases and clauses

*You can turn on the oven **either from work or in the car on the way home**.* (phrases)
***either before you leave work or as you drive home**.* (clauses)
*High-tech homes are good **not only in summer but also in winter**.* (phrases)
***not only because they are innovative but they also make life easier**.* (clauses)

A Rewrite the sentences using two-part conjunctions to combine phrases and clauses.

1. You can control the systems when you're at home. You can control them when you're somewhere else. (either . . . or)
2. With a sophisticated security system, you can monitor your house at work. You can monitor your house on vacation. (both . . . and)
3. A high-tech home can adjust the temperature when it gets cold outside. It can adjust the temperature after it warms up. (not only . . . but also)

About you

B Write three sentences about a home you'd like to live in. Use two-part conjunctions.

I would like to live in a home that has both a modern kitchen and a nice entertainment system. . . .

1 Clauses with prepositions and conjunctions + *-ing*

- Clauses with prepositions (e.g., *after, by*) + *-ing* or conjunctions (e.g., *while, when*) + *-ing* are common in writing. The subject of the *-ing* clause and the main clause should be the same.
  After completing** my masters, I felt pressured to study for a PhD.* (Formal: ***On / Upon completing . . .)
  ***By taking** extra classes, and **without telling** anyone, my sister was able to graduate early.*
  *Many students take on part-time work **while studying** for their masters.*
  *I changed careers and became a writer **after having worked** in accounting all my life.*

Complete the blog. Use *-ing* clauses with the words given.

(After / spend) ________ my college years at home, I was ready to set off into the world. So, (after / graduate) ________ , I flew to New York on a one-way ticket. (In / look back) ________, I feel I became truly independent (upon / board) ________ the plane. However, (while / stay) ________ with a friend for a week, I felt the initial excitement begin to wear off. Luckily, I had gotten in touch with her (before / leave) ________ home. But I didn't want to overstay my welcome. I also realized, (when / go) ________ for my first job interview, how much pressure I felt. I had to find a job *and* a place to live quickly. I soon found a paid internship at a design company (by / make) ________ dozens of phone calls, and shortly (after / start) ________ work, I was invited to rent a room in a colleague's apartment. (Since / come) ________ to New York, I have felt the pressure of city living, but I enjoy it. Of course, I've often felt homesick, but (by / make) ________ use of social media, I keep in touch with people. I also make sense of my experience of post-college life (through / write) ________ this blog.

2 Passive forms of participle and time clauses

- Passive participle clauses can start with a past participle or *having been* + past participle. Clauses that start with *being* + past participle are not common.
  ***Presented** with a chance to change careers, my father bought a café.* (= when he was presented)
  *My boss doesn't have many friends, **compared to** his co-workers.* (= if he is compared)
  ***Having been born** in the country, she found it hard to live in the city.* (= because she had been born)
- You can use prepositions or conjunctions before *being* + past participle or *having been* + past participle. Use only the conjunctions *when, while, as, if,* and *though* before a past participle.
  ***After being laid off,** most workers moved to other cities to find employment.* (more common)
  After having been laid off, . . . (less common)
  ***When told** that the company was closing, most people felt relieved.* (NOT ~~*After told*~~ . . .)

Rewrite the underlined clauses with a participle or time clause, as in the chart above. In two cases, you need to delete *and* from the sentence.

<u>Before he was elected</u>, a politician said that if more women managed corporations and more men stayed at home with their families, the world would be a better place. I heard the speech <u>while I was employed</u> at a bank, and I took it to heart. At the time, my wife, who held a higher position than me, and I were expecting our first child. <u>She was faced</u> with the prospect of interrupting her career, and she suggested that I should be the primary caregiver. So, <u>I was given</u> the chance to take care of our child, and I immediately agreed to do so. <u>As I had been raised</u> in a traditional family, I knew my parents would pressure me to pursue my career. Indeed, <u>when they were informed</u> of our decision, they were clearly disappointed. Twelve years later, I still believe I made the right choice. In fact, I feel fortunate, <u>if I am compared</u> to many of my friends. <u>When I'm asked</u> if I made the right choice, I say it's the best decision I ever made. My wife agrees. She is now the president of a large company.

1 More on *so* and *such*

- You can use *such* before some nouns to add emphasis. It means "big."
  It makes ***such a difference*** *to keep your desk neat. Mine was* ***such a mess.*** *I was* ***such an idiot.***
- With some nouns, *such* can refer forward to what will be mentioned.
  Organize your time in ***such a way*** *that you have time for a social life.*
- You can use *so* and *such* with determiners and pronouns: *so much / many / few / little; such a lot.*
  In my first semester, there were ***so many*** *parties that served pizza and soda. I ate* ***so much*** *(pizza) and drank* ***such a lot*** *(of soda) that I gained weight.*
- You can use *so much* as an adverb and before comparative adjectives and adverbs.
  I enjoyed college ***so much****. It was* ***so much better / more fun*** *than I expected.*
  The time went by ***so much more quickly*** *than I thought it would.*

Use *so* or *such* to complete the posts on a website about the challenges of marriage. Then write a post of your own on the topic of marriage using *so* or *such*.

1. There's no __________ **thing** as an easy marriage. It was __________ **much harder** at first than I imagined. I worked __________ **a lot**, and my husband and I spent __________ **little** time together that we almost broke up.
2. Getting married had __________ **an impact** on some of my friends. They had a lot of arguments at first, but my husband and I didn't have __________ **many**. You just have to take responsibility for making things work.
3. I've always loved my single life __________ **much** that I can't imagine getting married. Married life has been __________ **a disaster** for some of my friends, and I've seen __________ **many** of them get divorced.
4. I've enjoyed being married __________ **much** more than I thought. It's been __________ **a great experience**. My advice is to live your life in __________ **a way** that nothing takes precedence over your marriage.

2 More on *even* and *only*

- *Even* and *only* usually go after *be*, after an auxiliary verb, or before a main verb.
  Semesters ***are only*** *14 weeks.* ***I've even*** *made friends. I* ***only called*** *home a few times.*
- *Even* and *only* can also go before other words or phrases to add emphasis.

Nouns / pronouns	*The test was easy –* ***even weak students*** *passed.* ***Even I*** *got an A.*
Numbers	***Only one student*** *got a B.*
Adverbs	*I worked* ***even harder*** *in my last year. I missed class* ***only once****.*
Prepositions	*It was hard,* ***even in*** *the first week. It got easier* ***only after*** *spring break.*
Conjunctions	*I was tired* ***even before*** *classes started. I was tired* ***only because*** *I was sick.*

Note: *She* ***only missed*** *two classes because she was sick* can have two meanings.
You can make the meaning clear by moving the position of *only.*
She missed ***only*** *two classes because . . . She missed two classes* ***only*** *because . . .*

About you

Cross out the incorrect uses of *even* and *only*. Then answer the two questions about yourself.

A Do you remember your first job? I remember mine. I was nervous, **even** after the first month. But that's **only** because my boss **only** was so scary. She used to yell at everyone.

B Oh, that makes you feel **even** worse, if you have a boss like that.

A Yeah. I think **only** there was **only** one person that my boss liked. And **even** *he* **even** didn't like her. I **only** stayed in that job three weeks. Then I moved to another city. Have you ever had to move?

B Um, just once. We moved when I **only** was eight, and that was **only** because Dad got a new job. My parents **even** hadn't considered it before – they hadn't **even** been on a vacation.

1 More on the future perfect

- The future perfect describes events that at a future point will be in the past, or in a time leading up to that future point in time. It can emphasize the completion of the events.
  In two months, it will be winter and many birds ***will have migrated*** *south.* (The migration is complete.)
- Time expressions, especially with *by*, are often used with the future perfect to show the time by which an event will be complete, e.g., *by then, by that time, by the time (that) . . ., by 2030, by the end of the century, by the age of six, within 30 days, within a decade, within the next 20 years.*
  Within the next 10 years, *many species* ***will have become*** *extinct.*
- The future perfect has a passive form – *will have been* + past participle – but it is not very common.
  In the time it takes you to do this lesson, hundreds of sharks ***will have been killed****.*

Complete the time expressions with *by* or *within*. Then rewrite the verbs in bold using either the active or passive form of the future perfect.

_________ the time our children reach adulthood, hundreds of species **disappear** off the face of the planet. One study estimated that _________ 2050, 37 percent of terrestrial species **die out** or will be in danger of extinction. That is well over a third _________ the next 30 years.

Sea life is also in danger. _________ the time that sea levels rise 50 centimeters (about 20 inches), one-third of nesting beaches in the Caribbean **lose**, leading to the decline in turtle populations. _________ the end of this century, it is believed that seawater temperatures **rise** enough to affect the food supply of some ocean species. This impacts various species in different ways. For example, it is believed that _________ only a few decades, the reproductive cycle of the sperm whale **affect**, which threatens the very survival of the whale itself.

2 The future perfect for predictions and assumptions

- You can use the future perfect to state predictions or assumptions about the present or to say what you think has happened in the past. It suggests you are certain.
  No doubt you ***will have read*** *about the melting ice caps.*
  Many people ***will not have seen*** *the recent documentary about this.*
- The negative with *won't* with this meaning is mostly used in speaking and informal writing.
  "A lot of people ***won't*** *even* ***have heard*** *about it."*

Rewrite the underlined parts of the blog using the future perfect.

will not / won't have heard

It is unlikely that there is anyone who has not heard about the threat to certain species on the planet. No doubt you have reacted to the news that species such as polar bears are under threat. But what can we as individuals do? In recent years, perhaps you have noticed the appeals for help that come in the mail or that are on TV. They are certainly having an impact on my children. I'm sure that in addition to sending donations to various charities, you have heard about the "adopt an endangered animal" programs. I suspect what you haven't realized is how expensive these "adoptions" are. Not that I mind donating $50 for my child to adopt an orangutan or a Sumatran rhino. It's all for a good cause. And no doubt donations have saved some obscure species from the brink of extinction, and certainly the programs have motivated many children to become involved. What I hadn't expected was for a cuddly stuffed toy version to arrive in the mail. Now my daughter wants the entire collection, which is all very well – except there are more than 100 endangered species that she can sign up to help!

1 Formal prepositional expressions

- Some prepositional expressions are very frequent in academic writing. You can use them instead of more common prepositions to make your writing sound more formal.

after	*One desert spread* ***subsequent to / following*** *the introduction of new farming practices.*
before	*Delegates will meet* ***ahead of / in advance of / prior to*** *the conference.*
with	*Talks will take place* ***in conjunction with / alongside*** *an exhibition on deserts.* *Small mammals,* ***together with / along with*** *larger ones, survive in harsh climates.*
about	*There is concern* ***with respect to / with regard to / regarding / in relation to*** *agriculture.*
because of	*It is classified as a desert* ***owing to / in view of / on account of / given*** *its lack of rainfall.*

Circle the correct expressions to complete the paragraph. Then rewrite each sentence using an alternative expression from the chart above. More than one expression is possible.

Environmental concerns, especially **with regard to / in advance of** desertification, are growing. Desertification is a huge problem **prior to / with respect to** loss of habitats and agricultural land. **Given / Alongside** the problems that desertification causes, the United Nations adopted a convention in 1994. This convention proposed returning land to its original state (land rehabilitation) **in conjunction with / owing to** programs of sustainable land management. Many countries signed up to the convention **on account of / together with** the economic problems that desertification was causing. Projects that have emerged **prior to / following** the adoption of the convention include the mapping of desertification using satellite imagery **together with / on account of** a variety of educational programs. **In view of / Subsequent to** the severity of the issue, it appears that much more still needs to be done.

2 More on *the fact that*; prepositions + perfect forms

- The prepositional expressions *apart from, because of, besides, by virtue of, despite, due to, except for, including, in spite of, in view of, owing to, thanks to,* and *given* are often followed by *the fact that.*
  The Antarctic is classified as a desert ***in view of the fact that*** *it has low rainfall.*
  Despite the fact that *it is extremely cold, Antarctica is a desert.*
- Prepositions can be followed by *having* + past participle to refer to events in a period of time up to the present or up to a point in the past.
  The government takes credit ***for having initiated*** *a tree-planting program to halt desertification.*
  Agricultural practices were criticized ***as having been*** *partly responsible for the growth of deserts.*

Complete the sentences. In some, you need to add *the fact that*; in others, add *having*.

1. The Atacama desert is considered *the* driest region by virtue of ________ some parts have no rain.
2. Apart from ________ it is so dry, much of the land is also at high elevation.
3. It is surprising that over a million people are recorded as ________ settled there given ________ it is so arid.
4. Population centers developed in several areas despite ________ it is so inhospitable.
5. Teams of astronomers operate observatories in the desert due to ________ its skies are so clear.
6. Crops can now be grown owing to ________ farmers have developed irrigation systems.
7. Communities in northern Chile no longer import water into the region thanks to ________ they can now collect water from fog. Lives have improved.
8. A Canadian development team can be credited for ________ helped to develop this system.

1 Adverbs in present and past passive verb phrases

- In present and past passive verb phrases, adverbs usually go after the verb *be*. In negative statements, adverbs usually go after *not*. This is the most frequent position for most adverbs.

Simple present passive	Present continuous passive
*New discoveries are **apparently** made every day.*	*GPS software is **continually** being upgraded.*
Simple past passive	**Past continuous passive**
*Asbestos was **widely** used until the 1960s.*	*Alternatives were not **yet** being developed.*

- Some adverbs usually go before *not*, e.g.: *also, still, just, probably, certainly, reportedly,* attitude adverbs.
  *Alternatives were **simply** not developed until later.* *Alternatives were **still** not being developed.*
- Adverbs that describe the participle (e.g., to say "how" or "how much") often go before it.
  *Some inventions are not being **widely** reported or are being **completely** ignored by the media.*

Write the adverbs given into the underlined verb phrases.

Vaccinations are required for entry to kindergarten. (often) For many parents, it's a nuisance. Yet where would we be without them? One of the first vaccines was invented in 1776 by Edward Jenner, a British country doctor. (originally) A milkmaid was heard to say that she would never develop smallpox because she was infected with the cowpox virus. (reportedly / already) Jenner understood the significance, and thanks to him, a vaccine for smallpox was discovered. (fortunately)

Jenner's smallpox vaccine is being used today, but his work was not recognized. (still / initially) However, smallpox vaccines were used around the world and were even made compulsory by law, until 200 years later, when the disease was eradicated. (increasingly / eventually) The last case of smallpox was recorded in 1977. (finally)

While vaccines are not being developed for every disease, they have been approved for many life-threatening ailments. (currently / already) As a result, children are being protected from disease, which has to be anything *but* a nuisance. (effectively)

2 Adverbs in perfect verb phrases

- Adverbs usually go after *has / have / had*. Some can also go before for emphasis.
  In negative statements, adverbs usually go after *not*.
  *Some progress has **clearly** been made.* OR *. . . **clearly** has been made.* (more emphatic)
  *The difficulties of research had not **always** been understood.*
- Adverbs that describe the participle to say "how" or "how much" often go before it.
  *Scientists have not always been **widely** praised. Some have even been **sharply** criticized.*
- *Still* goes after *has / have / had*. In negative statements, *yet* goes after *not* or at the end of a clause.
  *Liquid water has **still** not been found on Mars. Liquid water has not **yet** been found on Mars.*
  OR *Liquid water has not been found on Mars **yet**.* (less formal)

Read the clues. Write the underlined words in the correct order. Can you guess the product?

1. A variation of this product widely been used has for millennia – since 4000 B.C.E., in fact.
2. A number of my friends said they thought that it had invented originally been by the Egyptians.
3. However, the first "recipe" for the product as we know it today been had created apparently by the Chinese. Historians say it used had been obviously to protect bronze mirrors in the second century.
4. In addition, records show that medicines had wrapped been carefully in it for safekeeping.
5. A replacement product yet been discovered not has, unless you consider computer technology.
6. The idea we can live without it not has materialized completely still, but will it ever be obsolete?

Exercise 2 Answer: Paper

1 Adverbs and past modal verb phrases

- In past modal verb phrases, adverbs like *probably, certainly,* and *definitely* often go before the modal.

Active	**Passive**
*He **never** should have tried to jump.*	*The jump **certainly** could have been stopped.*
*He **probably** should not have jumped.*	*It **probably** should not have been allowed.*

- Within the verb phrase, adverbs can go after the modal or after *have*. After the modal is more frequent.

*He should **never** have gone there.*	*It should **never** have been allowed.*
*Something bad could **easily** have happened.*	*Someone could **easily** have been killed.*

Read the post from a video website and the various comments. Put the words in a correct order. There is more than one correct answer.

In 2012, a young Russian base-jumper jumped off a tall electrical tower not knowing that his parachute wouldn't open. He crashed into the ground below and miraculously survived. He was able to walk again three months later after fracturing his legs and hip.

Comments

1. Not a good idea. He easily / have / could / died by jumping off that tower.
2. He also / have / been / might electrocuted!
3. His friends probably / should / have / allowed / not him to jump.
4. He checked / should / have / definitely his parachute before jumping!
5. He been / have / crippled / actually / could for life.
6. He looked nervous. He have / should / probably / followed his gut instinct and not jumped.
7. I never / watched / have / should this video. It was scary!

2 Questions with passive past modals

- Questions with passive past modals are not very common. In writing, they are often rhetorical.
  Would *these problems* ***have been avoided*** *if there had been more support?*
  Should *this trip* ***have been prevented****?*
  Could *more money* ***have been raised*** *in another way?*

Read the excerpt from an editorial news column. Then read the comments. Complete the questions in the passive form, using the verbs given.

The youngest British woman ever to climb Mount Everest was welcomed home by her family and friends this week. Such is the danger of climbing Everest that the return of any climber must be met with relief. However, the young Briton reported treacherous conditions. She had to climb past several badly-injured people and even some who had died. She had also experienced a dangerous 100-person "snarl up," as people rushed to the summit during a period of calm weather. It raises important questions about such dangerous expeditions. For example:

1. Should people have been allowed (allow) to climb in such treacherous conditions?
2. Could the injured climbers ______________ (help)?
3. Could more ______________ (do) to make the climb safer?
4. Would deaths ______________ (prevent) if people had shown better judgment?
5. In the past, should people rescued off the mountain ____________ (make) to pay for their rescue?
6. Should climbers ______________ (charge) for failing to help other injured climbers?

1 Pronouns and numbers in relative clauses

- Relative clauses can start with a pronoun (*both, each, much, neither, none, several,* etc.) + *of* or with numbers and quantity words (*half, 30 percent, the majority,* etc.) + *of.*
  In 2013, we launched two new products, ***neither of which*** *was successful. /* ***both of which*** *failed.*
  The company had four directors, ***each of whom*** *made a fortune. /* ***none of whom*** *stayed after the sale.*
  There are over 2 million businesses in Canada, ***the majority of which*** *have fewer than 100 employees.*
  One company has 500 employees, ***half of whom*** *are part-time.*

Common errors

Don't start these types of relative clauses with *which* or *whom.*
There are 100 companies, ***most of which*** *have one employee.* (NOT . . . ~~*which most of them*~~ *have* . . .)

Rewrite each pair of sentences from a report using a relative clause. You may delete words.

Consumers, most of whom are on tight budgets, are looking to save money when they shop.

1. Consumers are looking to save money when they shop. Most consumers are on tight budgets.
2. There are thousands of online coupon sites. The majority of these offer more or less the same thing.
3. So how do you know which sites to use or which information to trust? Much of it is misleading.
4. Our staff researched 10 options. Two of them are avid coupon users.
5. Two sites we researched had out-of-date coupons. Both are major players in the coupon business.
6. Our staff identified four more sites. None was easy to navigate.
7. On two sites, staff found much better deals than on other sites. Neither site is particularly well-known.
8. These two sites had coupons with discounts up to 30 percent. Each one specializes in grocery coupons.
9. Of the 10 sites we surveyed, three had too many distracting banner ads. Eighty percent offered email alerts.

2 Nouns in relative clauses

- Relative clauses can begin with a preposition, or a noun + preposition, + *which* or *whom.*
  Imagine a world ***in which*** *there is no profit motive and a staff* ***for whom*** *nothing is a problem.*
  The end-of-year report, ***a copy of which*** *was sent to the press, painted a gloomy picture.*
  The CEO of this company, ***a person for whom*** *I have great respect, just retired.*

Common errors

Don't start these types of relative clauses with *which* + noun.
We read the research, ***the results of which*** *were unclear.* (NOT ~~*which results were unclear.*~~)

Rewrite the underlined parts of the report as relative clauses that begin with the bold words.

in which no business fails.

Imagine a perfect economic environment that no business fails **in**. Unfortunately, the truth is that the rate that start-up companies fail **at** is high. The high failure rate, and **the main reasons for** this are given below, is concerning. Many owners, and start-up costs are high **for** them, are deterred by the risk of failure.

Reasons for failures of start-up companies

1. The frequency that new businesses fail **at** is high when they're started for the *wrong* reasons.
2. Many new business owners lack basic skills, and **the importance** of this cannot be underestimated. Above all, they need to be able to manage finances, and **an understanding** of this is critical.
3. The employees that the owner entrusts the business **to** often have the wrong skills.
4. A new business must have a website, and **the functions** can vary and **without** it the business will fail.
5. Many new business owners underestimate the prices that their products must sell **at** to make a profit.

1 *other, every other, other than*

- Before *other*, you can use *the, any, some, all, many, much, most, no, (a) few, every, this / that*, etc.
  One retailer outsells ***all other*** *stores.* ***No other*** *store can compete.* ***Few other*** *stores do as well.*
  There is ***no other*** *business news. If* ***any other*** *information comes to light, it will be reported.*
- You can also use these words: *several, various, numerous, whole, certain, countless.*
  Online shopping is ***a whole other*** *problem for small retailers. There are* ***several other*** *threats too.*
- Every *other* can mean "alternate" and is often used with time words (*day, week, year*, etc.).
  We go to the grocery store ***every other weekend.***
- *Other than* means "except" or "apart from."
  Salesclerks need to speak a language ***other than*** *English.*

Common errors

Don't use *others* before a plural noun.
Retailers face ***other*** *threats.*
(NOT ~~*others threats*~~)

Use *other, others,* or *every other* to complete the sentences in this business report.

1. While many retailers are struggling, one electronics retailer outperforms all ______ stores. No ______ company attracts such a loyal consumer base. In fact, many consumers will *not* be seen with products ______ than these smartphones or tablets, which must be the envy of most ______ retailers.
2. Selling print magazines has been difficult in recent years. One magazine recently announced that it will now publish only online, and numerous ______ magazines are considering doing the same. Many ______ have simply gone out of business.
3. Maintaining sales is a problem for any small business, but supporting online sales is a whole ______ issue. Some simply don't create user-friendly sites, while some ______ often don't know how to make their sites visible on the Web.
4. While some stores are concerned about the loss of sales to online retailers, certain ______ stores are tackling the issue head-on. One retailer lets customers pick up goods that they ordered online at the store the same day. It's a huge advantage over all ______ competing stores, which deliver their goods only ______ week.

2 More on *another*

- *Another* can mean "an additional" or "an alternative." You can use it before a singular countable noun, the pronoun *one*, numbers, and *few*, or as a pronoun instead of a singular count noun.
  I bought ***another*** *sweater. I liked it so much I bought* ***another (one)*** *in* ***another*** *color.*
  I actually bought ***another three*** *sweaters. In* ***another few*** *weeks, I'll buy some more.*

Read the blog. Find seven more places where you can replace words with *another*.

I recently bought a sweater online, but when it arrived, it didn't fit. I decided to order ~~a different~~ another one in a different size, and return the first sweater. It was a long process. I called customer service, and they promised to send me a return label. Only they didn't. I emailed them, made a second call, and then sent an additional email. Finally, I got the return label and went to the post office. I had to make a further trip, however, as I had forgotten to wrap the sweater in the original packaging. Now I have to wait an additional five days before it ships. I'll have to wait an extra couple of weeks before the refund appears on my credit card statement. Meanwhile, I ordered a new sweater, which was out of stock. Next time I'll just go to the store.

Illustration credits

19: (cartoon) Liza Donnelly/Cambridge University Press; **25:** (cartoon) Liza Donnelly/Cambridge University Press; **31:** (cartoon) Liza Donnelly/Cambridge University Press; **45:** (cartoon) Liza Donnelly/Cambridge University Press; **57:** (cartoon) Liza Donnelly/Cambridge University Press; **67:** (cartoon) Liza Donnelly/Cambridge University Press;

Photography credits

Back cover: © vovan/Shutterstock; **10:** (top right from left to right) © Leaf/Veer, © Amy Johansson/Shutterstock, (middle row, left to right) © Blend Images/Shutterstock, © Yuri Arcurs/Shutterstock, © amana images inc./Alamy, (bottom row, left to right) © Felix Mizioznikov/Shutterstock, © Svetlana Yudina/Shutterstock, © Bill Bachmann/Alamy; **11:** © Luminis/Shutterstock; **12:** © Datacraft - Sozaijiten/Alamy; **13:** (top to bottom) © Bryn Colton/Getty, © Getty Images; **14:** Cambridge University Press; **15:** (top) Cambridge University Press; (middle from top to bottom) © Andrey Sukhachev/Shutterstock, © Peter Firus/iStockphoto, © Thinkstock; **16:** (clockwise from top right) © Portrait Essentials/Alamy, © JTB MEDIA CREATION, Inc./Alamy, © Getty Images, (background) © Sharon Day/Shutterstock, © MaxyM/Shutterstock; **17:** © Andersen Ross/Media Bakery; **20:** (top right from left to right) © Thinkstock, A-R-T/Shutterstock, © Warren Goldswain/Shutterstock, © Warren Goldswain/Shutterstock, (middle from left to right) © DreamPictures/Getty, © AVAVA/Shutterstock, © lithian/Shutterstock, © michaeljung/Shutterstock, (background) © Amanda Rohde/iStockphoto; **21:** (bottom right) © Ignard Karel Maria ten Have/iStockphoto, © Tolga TEZCAN/istockphoto; **22:** © Javier Pierini/Getty; **23:** © John Kasawa/Shutterstock; **24:** Cambridge University Press; **25:** Cambridge University Press; **26:** (background) © Shutterstock; **27:** (bottom right) © Robert Stainforth/Alamy, (background) © file404/Shutterstock; **30:** (top right from left to right) © Jacek_Kadaj/Shutterstock, © Solphoto/Shutterstock, © Thinkstock, (bottom right) © OJO Images Ltd/Alamy, © PhotoAlto/Frederic Cirou/Getty, © Ben Bloom/Getty, © Eric Milos/Shutterstock; **32:** © Sam Edwards/Getty; **33:** (bottom right) © Jose Luis Pelaez/Media Bakery, © Konstantin Chagin/Shutterstock; **34:** Cambridge University Press; **35:** (top) Cambridge University Press, (bottom) © Thinkstock; **36:** (middle right) © The Photo Works/Alamy, (bottom) © Lew Robertson/Getty; **37:** © moodboard/Alamy; **42:** (top right from left to right) © Marcelo Sanchez/istockphoto, © Troy Kennedy/istockphoto, © IrinaK/Shutterstock, (middle, left to right) © Arto Hakola/Shutterstock, © John Czenke/Shutterstock, © Martin Ruegner/Getty Images/RF; **43:** (top to bottom) © Jodi Jacobson/istockphoto, © Olga Khoroshunova/Fotolia, © Dan Whobrey/istockphoto; **44:** (top row, left to right) © Danner Bradshaw/istockphoto, © dirk ercken/istockphoto, © forcdan/Fotolia, © Bastos/Fotolia, (background) © Beboy/Fotolia; **45:** © Armin Rose/istockphoto; **46:** Cambridge University Press; **47:** (top) Cambridge University Press, (bottom) © Warwick Lister-Kaye/istockphoto; **48:** (clockwise from top right) © Elzbieta Sekowska/Shutterstock, © Serge Vero/Alamy, © Rich Carey/Shutterstock, (inset) © DEA/A. DAGLI ORTI/Getty Images, (background) © bgfoto/iStockphoto, © Nataliya Hora/iStockphoto; **49:** (left to right) © greg801/iStockphoto, © Ron Yue/Alamy, © Peter Nguyen/iStockphoto, © Glenn Bo/iStockphoto; **52:** (top right from left to right) © Prixnews/Alamy, © cosmin4000/istockphoto, © Yuri Arcurs/Fotolia, (middle from left to right) © Kokhanchikov/Shutterstock, © Nikola Bilic/Shutterstock, © D. Hurst/Alamy, © Dja65/Shutterstock, (background) © Paul Cowan/iStockphoto; **53:** (top to bottom) © ft2010/Fotolia, © Andrew Johnson/istockphoto, © Thinkstock; **54:** (middle left) © George Paul/iStockphoto, (middle right) © Andrew Milligan/PA Wire/AP Images, (background) © sunil menon/iStockphoto; **55:** © Kristen Ulmer; **56:** (middle left) Cambridge University Press, (rocket) © Tomasz Szymanski/Shutterstock; **57:** (top) Cambridge University Press, (bottom left to right) © Antagain/istockphoto, © Igor Prole/istockphoto; **58:** (clockwise from top left) © Getty Images, © Maxx-Studio/Shutterstock, © Ocean/Corbis/RF, © arka38/Shutterstock, © Stepan Popov/istockphoto, (background) © Thinkstock; **59:** (top row, left to right) © Hugh Threlfall/Alamy, © keith morris/Alamy, © Michael Poor/Cambridge University Press, © iofoto/istockphoto; **60:** (top to bottom) © National Geographic Image Collection/Alamy, © Dan Vincent/Alamy; **62:** (top right from left to right) © Anna Bryukhanova/iStockphoto, © Thinkstock, © Thinkstock, (middle right) © Scott Olson/Getty Images, (background) © Thinkstock; **63:** © Thinkstock; **64:** © kali9/istockphoto; **65:** © franckreporter/istockphoto; **66:** Cambridge University Press; **67:** Cambridge University Press; **68:** (bottom right) © DNY59/iStockphoto, (background) © zokara/iStockphoto; **69:** © Mikkel William Nielsen/iStockphoto; **71:** © Don Bayley/istockphoto.

Text credits

The authors and publishers acknowledge the following sources of copyright material and are grateful for the permissions granted. While every effort has been made, it has not always been possible to identify the sources of all the material used, or to trace all copyright holders. If any omissions are brought to our notice, we will be happy to include the appropriate acknowledgements on reprinting.

15 Statistics listed at: http://thefuturebuzz.com/.
26 Rogers, E.M. 2003. *Diffusion of Innovations* (5th Edition). New York: Free Press.
28 "World Internet Penetration Rates by Geographic Regions – 2012" and "Internet Users in the World, Distribution by World Regions – 2012," Copyright © 2000 – 2012, Miniwatts Marketing Group. All rights reserved.
48 "Sharkskin," from research by Anthony Brennan, PhD, professor of biomedical engineering, University of Florida.
68 Information used with the permission of http://thenetwork.cisco.com/.
80 Data used by permission of Pew Research Center's Internet & American Life Project.
136 Information on women in the workplace used from the U.S. Census Bureau (www.census.gov/hhes/socdemo/education/data/cps/2010/tables.html) and from a 2009 study conducted by N. Scott Taylor of the University of New Mexico.

Corpus

Development of this publication has made use of the Cambridge English Corpus (CEC). The CEC is a computer database of contemporary spoken and written English, which currently stands at over one billion words. It includes British English, American English, and other varieties of English. It also includes the Cambridge Learner Corpus, developed in collaboration with the University of Cambridge ESOL Examinations. Cambridge University Press has built up the CEC to provide evidence about language use that helps produce better language teaching materials.